Southern FICTIONS

Contemporary Arts Museum
Houston, Texas

August 2 – September 4, 1983
Essays by William A. Fagaly and Dr. Monroe K. Spears

John Alexander
David Bates
Donald Beason
Derek Boshier
William Christenberry
Rebecca Davenport
James Drake
William Eggleston
Vernon Fisher
Roy Fridge
Robert Gordy
Jimmy Jalapeeno
Alexa Kleinbard
Clarence John Laughlin

Ken Dawson Little
Ed McGowin
Melissa Miller
Nic Nicosia
Francie Rich
Art Rosenbaum
Julian Schnabel
Lee N. Smith III
Gael Stack
Earl Staley
Richard Stout
James Surls
Russell Warren
Susan Whyne

The exhibition has been funded through a generous grant from
Imperial Sugar Company with additional support from
Gulf Oil Corporation and Mischer Corporation.

The catalogue is made possible through the **Contemporary
Arts Publication Fund** established by The Charles Engelhard
Foundation in May 1982 with additional support from The Brown
Foundation, Inc., Houston, Texas and The Arch and Stella Rowan
Foundation, Inc.

Library of Congress Card Catalogue Number 83-70898
ISBN 0-936080-11-6

This publication has been prepared in conjunction with the
exhibition *Southern Fictions* organized by Linda L. Cathcart
and Marti Mayo for the Contemporary Arts Museum, Houston,
Texas. August 2 – September 4, 1983

Table of Contents

Lenders to the Exhibition

John Alexander, New York City
David Bates, Dallas, Texas
Donald Beason, Nacogdoches, Texas
Dennis Bieber
Derek Boshier, Houston, Texas
William Christenberry, Washington, D.C.
Robin Cronin, Houston, Texas
Steve Dennie, Dallas, Texas
James Drake, El Paso, Texas
William Eggleston, Memphis, Tennessee
Roy Fridge, Victoria, Texas
Helen and Rick Gardner, Houston, Texas
Ian Glennie, Houston, Texas
Robert Gordy, New Orleans, Louisiana
Robert K. Hoffman, Dallas, Texas
Fredericka Hunter, Houston, Texas
Renée Jacobs, Morristown, New Jersey
Jimmy Jalapeeno, Austin, Texas
Mr. and Mrs. I.H. Kempner III, Houston, Texas
Alexa Kleinbard, Havana, Florida
Robert E. Kinnaman, Houston, Texas
Ken Dawson Little, Norman, Oklahoma
Ed McGowin, New York City
Betty Moody, Houston, Texas
Nic Nicosia, Dallas, Texas
Martin Owen, Houston, Texas
Hanoj and Myrna Perez, North Miami Beach, Florida
Brian A. Ramaekers, Houston, Texas
Francie Rich, Covington, Louisiana
Mr. and Mrs. Richard C. Roeder, Houston, Texas
Joanna Rogers, Dallas, Texas
Art Rosenbaum, Athens, Georgia
Julian Schnabel, New York City
Lee N. Smith III, Dallas, Texas
Gael Stack, Houston, Texas
Earl Staley, Houston, Texas
John Stephenson, Houston, Texas
Richard Stout, Houston, Texas
James Surls, Splendora, Texas
Michael Tracy, San Ygnacio, Texas
Russell Warren, Davidson, North Carolina
Susan Whyne, Austin, Texas
Bob Wilson, Houston, Texas

Delahunty Gallery, Dallas, Texas
DW Gallery, Dallas, Texas
Charles Cowles Gallery, New York City
Barbara Gladstone Gallery, New York City
Iolas/Jackson Gallery, New York City
Phyllis Kind Gallery, New York City
Janie C. Lee Gallery, Houston, Texas
Meredith Long and Company, Houston, Texas
Middendorf Gallery, Washington, D.C.
Moody Gallery, Houston, Texas
Texas Gallery, Houston
Watson/de Nagy and Company, Houston, Texas

Atlantic Richfield Company, Dallas, Texas
The Museum of Fine Arts, Houston, Texas

Acknowledgements

A survey exhibition representing a diverse and geographically scattered group of artists requires timely cooperation and support from Museum patrons, the institution's staff, the lenders, the artists and their dealers.

First, as always our thanks are due to both the individual and institutional lenders who have made *Southern Fictions* possible. Their willingness to share valuable and loved works of art with us and our audience for the duration of the exhibition deserves our deepest appreciation.

One of the greatest rewards of a show such as this is the personal contact we establish with each artist. This contact has enriched us and been particularly helpful. Each artist has cooperated generously with us assuring not only the successful installation of the exhibition but also the timely completion of the accompanying catalogue.

Galleries in Dallas, Houston, New Orleans, New York and Washington, D.C. have provided documentation on the artists' careers, photographs of works of art and they have facilitated efficient and safe transportation of the works to Houston. Diana Block, D W Gallery, Dallas, Texas; Steve Dennie and Barry Whistler, Delahunty Gallery, Dallas, Texas; Janie C. Lee and Gene Binder, Janie C. Lee Gallery, Houston, Texas; Meredith Long and Ben Crump, Meredith Long and Company, Houston, Texas; Betty Moody and Lisa Barkley, Moody Gallery, Houston, Texas; Fredericka Hunter, Ian Glennie and Kathleen Crane, Texas Gallery, Houston; Marvin Watson and Clint Wilhour, Watson/de Nagy and Company, Houston, Texas; Barbara Muniot, Galerie Simonne Stern, New Orleans, Louisiana; Jean Auberbach, Auberbach Fine Art, New York City; Barbara Gladstone, Barbara Gladstone Gallery, New York City; Chuck Helsley, Iolas/Jackson Gallery, New York City; Phyllis Kind, Phyllis Kind Gallery, New York City; and Chris Middendorf, Middendorf Gallery, Washington, D.C. all have helped bring the exhibition to its finished state.

The dedicated staff of the Contemporary Arts Museum has performed with its usual professional and diligent skill in accomplishing the various aspects of the exhibition and publication. Timothy N. Walters, publications and public information officer, has edited this catalogue and overseen its production accommodating a series of strenuous deadlines. Emily Croll, registrar, has arranged the preparation and the transportation of the loans, and head preparator Michael J. Barry and assistant preparator Clay Henley have installed the exhibition. Mary Cullather, curatorial secretary has typed portions of the manuscript and research assistant Lisa Schoyer ably prepared the artists' biographies and helped with many of the project's details during her temporary assignment at the Museum.

Valuable and insightful essays have been contributed to this publication by William A. Fagaly, Assistant Director for Art, New Orleans Museum of Art, Louisiana, and Dr. Monroe K. Spears, Libbie Shearn Moody Professor of English, Rice University, Houston. Each has brought great knowledge and a special point of view to the project, and we are deeply grateful. Mr. Fagaly is a long-time resident of New Orleans and is an astute observer of Southern culture and its art. Dr. Spears is a long-time resident of Houston whose field is modern literature. He is the recent recipient of an honorary doctorate of letters degree from the University of the South at Sewanee, Mississippi. He was previously the editor of the *Sewanee Review*.

We are particulary grateful to the sponsors whose financial support has, in the most direct way, made this project possible. The exhibition has been funded through a very generous grant from Imperial Sugar Company with additional support provided by Gulf Oil Corporation and Mischer Corporation. The catalogue has been made possible through the *Contemporary Arts Publication Fund* established by The Charles Engelhard Foundation in May 1982 with additional support from The Brown Foundation, Inc., Houston, Texas and The Arch and Stella Rowan Foundation, Inc. These major contributions have allowed us to present the exhibition and to execute ever more ambitious exhibition catalogues, and we are delighted to be joined in our efforts by the perceptive and generous individuals and corporations named above.

Linda L. Cathcart
Director

Marti Mayo
Curator

Introduction

Presented in the context of a continuing effort to exhibit and document the art of this region, *Southern Fictions* began as a show concentrating on a few artists much as had the 1981 exhibition *4 Painters: Jones, Smith, Stack, Utterback.* After looking at the work of artists who seemed clearly focused and thinking about an overall concept, we determined that much of the art we felt was strong and mature shared certain characteristics. We tried to identify what these shared elements were and why the work "looked" dissimilar but "felt" the same in many ways, and we began to define what intrigued us: a certain boldness of both idea and technique often combined with highly charged color, definite emotional content often unabashedly personal, a certain propensity on the part of the artist to point out life's paradoxes by the use of a sometimes surreal space and imagery and an eccentric, original and yet humanist rendering of the figure. We found in our researches and conversations that we were not the first to have remarked on this similarity in feeling or outlook by Southern artists. It had often been remarked upon in the prefaces or forewords of other publications which accompanied surveys or juried exhibitions from this region.

As our investigation proceeded, it became evident that these Southern characteristics were found in the work of a diverse group of artists working in a variety of styles and media. Some of these artists were born and reared in this region and have pursued their entire professional career here. Others grew up or were educated in the South and some only spent brief periods of time in the region and have adopted certain attitudes which place their work within the framework described by this exhibition. Still others have moved to the area to teach or because the life-style is amenable or certain attitudes appeal to their sensibility.

These artists have a shared vision or attitude toward the real or mythic heritage of the South. Unlike artists who live and work in areas with less concentrated and more diverse traditions, such as New York City, Chicago or Los Angeles, the artists in this exhibition are tied to a cultural ethos that sometimes assumes legendary status. Among those national figures who characterize, contribute to and who are a product of this culture of mythic proportions are writers such as William Faulkner and Tennessee Williams and artists such as Robert Rauschenberg and Jasper Johns.

Some of the most expressionistic figurative work found in *Southern Fictions* appears related to the Neo-Expressionist or New Figuration painting which currently is receiving critical attention in the galleries and museums of New York City and Europe. Yet, while the work may *look* alike, its origins are very different.

The figurative and expressionist tradition in the South is long-standing, seemingly indigenous and is often a response to a cultural milieu concerned with or in reaction to, for instance, the home, family, the land. Similar work from the North is, in contrast, a return to overt content and a redefinition or rethinking of formal elements redirected to more expressive ends. This is not to say that Southern artists have been unsophisticated in their use of formal elements, but rather that they have used these primarily toward the expression of more personal ends.

The debate of the relative value of "regionalism" is ever-present and on-going. This exhibition does not attempt to address that debate, but rather to propose that some art from the southern United States has common themes and roots as a result of the culture itself.

Since much of the art presented here contains an overt or implied narrative, and since those of us from other parts of the country historically have been intrigued and influenced by Southern art forms such as music, literature and drama, we wanted to identify and relate this art to those other forms of expression.

Such relationships between the arts — particularly the visual arts and literature made it seem natural to invite Dr. Monroe K. Spears who teaches at Rice University and whose field is modern literature to contribute his thoughts to this publication on the common attitudes shared by Southern art and Southern literature. This essay is complemented by that written by William A. Fagaly who has, for several years, overseen regional surveys presented at the museum in New Orleans. His insightful essay comments on artists included in the exhibition as well as on the visual aspects of Southern life and culture.

The South has a unique and viable visual arts tradition, even if it is less identified and documented than other art forms native to the region. Our aim in organizing this exhibition and presenting this publication is to begin a discussion of this tradition and initiate a dialogue between this work and the art from other regions of the country.

Linda L. Cathcart
Director

Marti Mayo
Curator

Southern Fictions by William A. Fagaly

It has been said that what Tennessee Williams and William Faulkner wrote was neither artistic nor creative but strict reportage. This outrageous exaggeration concerning the oeuvres of two of the South's twentieth-century literary giants is, of course, absurd. While admittedly simplistic, the point is that art — any good art — is, among other things, a reflection of the times and place in which it has been produced and Williams and Faulkner are "guilty on all counts."

Before examining the recent works of artists living in the Southern region, one is first obliged to consider briefly the environment and attitudes particular to the area. It is recognized that artists do not work in a vacuum but consciously or unconsciously rely on the external signifiers to shape their ideas and, in turn, their creative output. A review of such influences can provide a clearer understanding of the Southern aesthetic.

Admittedly it is difficult to speak in generalities about the territory with its multi-faceted disposition and culture. For example, even though the South has, for the most part, a rural heritage and identification, it is a mixed tradition. This is manifested by the soybean and peanut dirt farms worked by the rednecks of Georgia, Mississippi and Alabama which are quite different from the rice and sugar-cane fields of Louisiana "coonasses" or the tobacco agriculture produced by the Carolina, Kentucky and Tennessee hillbillies. And again the horse farms of Virginia, Kentucky, and Tennessee owned by country gentlemen do not compare with the cattle ranches in Texas run by cowboys. Chiefly such divergences can be attributed to variances in climate and topography and to the different European origins of the people: Spain and France claimed Louisiana, Texas and Florida while Germans and Scotch-Irish immigrants from the British Isles settled in Mississippi, Alabama, Georgia, Virginia, Kentucky, Tennessee and the Carolinas.

The South has a strong sense of place and obsession with the earth. Indigenous live oaks, Spanish moss, water hyacinths and the ever present kudzu flourish; armadillos, 'possums, snakes and raccoons populate the countryside. The embodiment of this identification with the land is the prestigious area known as "The Delta," a rich farmland in North Mississippi traditionally defined and acknowledged as beginning in the lobby of the Peabody Hotel in Memphis and extending south to Catfish Row in Vicksburg. Integral to this sense of place is a veneration of the past and tradition which emphasizes resolute family loyalty and ancestral respect and commitment. Fraternal "good ole boy" or Texas macho attitudes are popular, while deep pride and nostalgia for things that no longer exist, for grander times, prevail throughout the region. The gentlemenly nineteenth-century custom of dueling for one's honor with pistols has been replaced today with drag races. Southerners today refer to the War Between the States, while Northerners call it the Civil War; the difference is a matter of attitude. Southerners steadfastly claim the conflict was not, as believed by Northerners, an act of civil disobedience on their part but a disagreement over the interpretation of certain basic constitutional principles.

Latin cultures and tropical environments tend to "breed" a more volatile society given to strong expression and vibrant color, and the South fits this description. The preoccupation with place, past and tradition is laden with an emotional intensity equalled by the prevailing fervor for sex and religion. Southern belief systems range from the followers of such divergent religious leaders as Jerry Falwell, Edgar Cayce and Martin Luther King. Beside Catholics and myriad Baptist offshoots (Free Will, Independent, Southern, American), heretical groups include Blue Ridge snake cults, Louisiana voodoo, Foursquare Gospel, Charismatics and palm readers. Present day debates over creationism in Louisiana recall the 1925 Scopes "monkey" trial which challenged the teachings of Darwin's theory of evolution in the classrooms of Tennessee. In regards to sex, Southerners take a certain secret pride in "skeletons in the closet," while taboo and unorthodox sexual habits seem to be practiced with greater frequency and acceptability than elsewhere.

Uncontrolled emotional release resulting in violence and tragedy has a particular place in the Southern ethos. Sadistic torture, hangings and "mad houses" are but a few examples. The curious phenomenon of violence for pleasure takes the form of cock fights, dog fights, "coon on a log" or hunting and trapping for sport. Interest in the sensational and fantastic, be it carney and freak shows or roadside reptile farms, is indicative of a people who respond with zeal to external stimuli.

The Southland has a unique lifestyle. Many of the idioms come from the black culture with its roots in Central and West Africa and the Caribbean. The pace tends to be slower with a more easy going, laissez-faire posture. The Scarlett O'Hara "I will think about that tomorrow" or the Latin mañana attitudes predominate. A common, often repeated, response to an inquiry about a long delayed delivery of an ordered service or product is, "it's on the truck."

There is a tendency toward self-gratification which manifests itself in a passion for eating, drinking, loving and partying, not found elsewhere with such fervor and gusto as in the South. This hedonistic outlook is reflected in many ways, including the desire for not one, but two, first names such as Billy Bob, Jimmy Joe or Sue Carol. On the other hand shortened nicknames like Dodie, Bubba, and Lulu are common.

For the Southerner food becomes a passionate indulgence. It is commonly said that in New Orleans a person spends half of his time eating and the other half talking about it. The list of foods particularly prepared in the South seems endless: cured ham, red-eye gravy, biscuits, spoon bread, hominy grits, chess pie, grillades, red beans and rice, jambalaya, gumbo, hush puppies, chitlins, greens, key lime and pecan pie. Only in the South can one find people having a Coke for breakfast or pre-sweetened iced tea served in restaurants.

Another indulgent appetite is for a native music focusing on the blues, jazz, country, western, rockabilly, sacred harp, gospel, cajun and bluegrass centering around the music centers of Austin, Nashville, Memphis, New Orleans, Macon and Muscle Shoals.

There is a penchant for congregating for social interchange whether it be at church, the hardware store, sidewalk or park bench, or highway dance halls and beer taverns. Sitting around in groups exchanging stories or ''bullshitting each other'' with lies and exaggeration is popular in the rural South. This oral narrative tradition is the basis for the South's strong literary heritage. The rollcall of twentieth-century authors who write about the Southern experience reads like a *Who's Who* of American literature. It is interesting to note that there are an equal number of men and women who come to mind: Carson McCullars, Flannery O'Connor, Eudora Welty, Walker Percy, Tennessee Williams, William Faulkner, Truman Capote, James Dickey, Anne Rice, James Agee, Lillian Hellman, Erskine Caldwell and Robert Penn Warren.

The South has long suffered an inferiority complex, and its visual artists are no exception. The artists' apparent lack of recognition by the bellwethers of the art world (i.e., New York City) is due, in part, to their comparative isolation from the mainstream. This results in a painfully slow response to their work, which is even

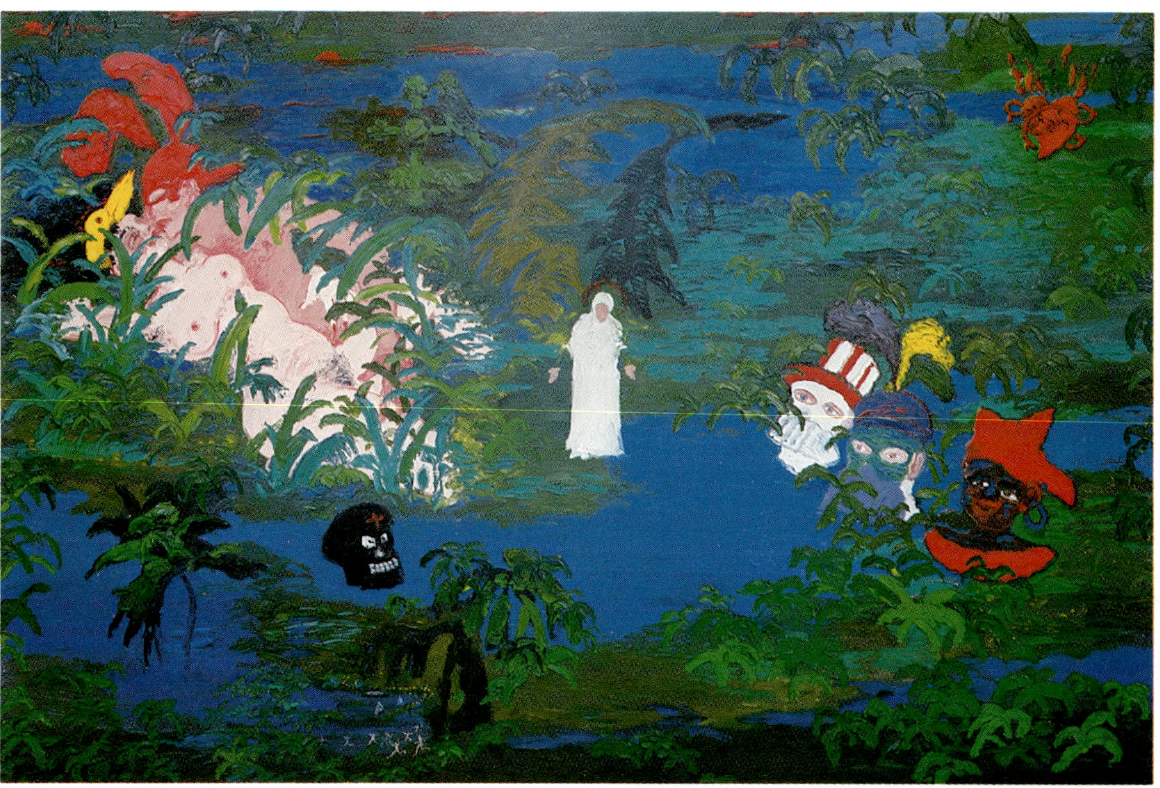

Derek Boshier

Mysteries — New Orleans 1983
Oil on canvas
88½ × 134"
Courtesy the artist and
Texas Gallery, Houston

then often negative. By and large the art capital doyens have long scorned the art being produced in the South. A notable exception was Robert Doty, formerly a curator at the Whitney Museum of American Art, who was one of the first to recognize that something was going on of interest in the Bay Area of California, Chicago and the South. His two landmark exhibitions addressing this non-formalist based art, *Human Concern, Personal Torment* (1969) and *Extraordinary Realities* (1973) were received in New York with disdain and hostility.

Not only do large numbers of artists now feel it is no longer necessary to live in New York City to make it, but there is also something to be said for the Southern artists' desire to live and work near their sources. A look at the work in the exhibition will reveal that importance. Vernon Fisher was born in Texas, and frequently exhibits nationally, but chooses to live in Fort Worth. His multi-media painted wall constructions are reminiscent of another Texas-born artist Robert Rauschenberg's combines. Depicting invented anecdotes, personal incidents, allegories and ideas embodying nostalgia, mystery, social foibles and wry humor, Fisher's work often has an overlaying of text with perforated stencil letter forms on the pictorial image, not necessarily with a readily apparent direct relationship between them. The contents of many of the tales lack any particular regional reference or context while the storytelling act remains a truly Southern characteristic. The manner in which Fisher relates his written yarns, creating a confusion between reality and fiction, reflects on the popular Southern tradition of embellishment of the truth or hyperbole. In the same vein as the ambiguity of content and technique, the combination of images and objects in the individual piece lacks any discernible common bond, but becomes specific private symbols, occasionally with a regional identification. In spite of this stratum of disparity, there remains a cohesiveness to the whole which betrays a complex calculation to interjoin elements and content much like the indigenuous literature.

Like Fisher, photographer Nic Nicosia also joins intricate visual and storytelling elements into a coherent whole. He literally constructs the sets and props, directs the actor/figures in the theatrical scenes and then shoots his "domestic dramas" with the camera. The undisguised artificality of these staged situations poses an ambiguity between reality and fantasy. Drawing upon everyday and personal experience with multi-focused plots and sub-plots, Nicosia's contrived one-scene narrations have a cartoonlike character and utilize humor on two levels. The dreamed-up stories, satirical in content, apply amusing fool-the-eye tricks and clever virtuosity.

This surreal illusionism is quite different from the romantic surrealism found in the large body of work of New Orleans photographer, Clarence John Laughlin, one of the elder statesmen of the Southern aesthetic and of the medium as a fine art form. In considering his production, which began in the 1930s, it is often ignored that Laughlin has always considered himself a writer first, then a photographer. For him the images illustrate his written word, but in fact the two support each other. His work, which could be categorized as Southern gothic, is about the occult, animism, fantasy, dreams, perceptions, isolation, death, memories, illusion, demons, phantoms, metaphysics, apparitions, poetry, fairies, visions. This admitted "extreme romantic" explains his constant themes and preoccupations as "the mystery of time, the magic of light, the enigma of reality — and their relationships." The rich and varied imagery includes natural forms (trees, dead birds, cobwebs), architecture (decaying Greek Revival plantations, New Orleans raised cemeteries, Victorian houses), costumed figures in ruined environments. The artist has sorted out his captioned photographs into categories with such descriptive titles as *Fantasy in Old New Orleans, The Images of the Lost, Poems of the Inner World* and *New Anatomies.* Laughlin's photographs have often been compared with the writings of Lafcadio Hearn whose work he greatly admires. In short, Laughlin's contribution has to be considered as one progenitor of this Southern viewpoint and epitomizes its direction.

Through site-specific, theatrical environments Donald Beason creates moods, evokes feelings using an assortment of found objects, discarded dolls and toy animals, full-size plaster mannikins of humans and horses wrapped in gauze, and crudely cut-out animals reminiscent of folk sculpture. The composite objects, usually viewed through layers of screen which diffuse the light and blur the edges, transmit a single idea not necessarily related to the meanings of the individual components. Often dreamlike and full of mystery and drama like Laughlin's photographs, these haunting sculptural tableaux, concerned with private myths, possess romantic tendencies through their emotional impact coupled with surrealist qualities.

Ed McGowin's two works in the exhibition are *Robbery*, pertaining to the holdup of a liquor store, and *Rescue*, which is about a dog saving a man from drowning. These wall-relief constructions are full of emotion encompassing human tragedy, conflict, and violence. The media incorporated varies from the look of anonymous industrial machine fabrication to individual hand craftsmanship depending on the most effective means to convey a particular expressive quality. McGowin's sculptures are based on his own invented stories, founded on the truth and frequently drawing upon his Mississippi background. (In Jackson and Hattiesburg he has dedicated two large *Inscape* structures respectively to fellow Mississippi littérateurs William Faulkner and Eudora Welty.) In *Robbery* there is a clear sequential narration of the drama from (a) setting up the scene and situation, to (b) the unfolding and buildup, to (c) the climax and denouement. Windowlike or shadowbox elements, into which the viewer peers, serve as framing devices to contain the progression of individual episodes or, as it were, chapters or acts.

Susan Whyne's large, painted canvasses describe a world suggestive of cheap, pulp romance novels and daytime TV soap operas. The raw emotions of guilt, lust, passion, grief, greed, gluttony and hate spill forth through torrid embraces, swirling water and turbulent clouds, exotic vegetation and women in tight fitting strapless gowns with Latin ruffled shirts. Cheap overstuffed moderne furniture, bric-a-brac statues, magazines, TV's and junk food clutter these lascivious melodramas highlighted and compressed through manipulation of *non sequitur* space and placement of objects. This outrageous outpouring of uncontrolled emotion coupled with the surreal environment give this work a total Southern identification.

Derek Boshier is an Englishman who has been in Houston for the past few years. His large paintings are concerned with his own personal viewpoints as an observer of customs and lifestyle peculiar to the South. Issues with strong social and political implications are favorite subjects. There is an interest in portraying identifiable public figures known for their emotional and passionate beliefs, such as Lech Walesa and Southerners Lee Harvey Oswald and Ku Klux Klan members. Other works involve topics of personal involvement such as his impressions and reactions following his first visit to New Orleans or portraits of his close friend — actor and rock star David Bowie. In the same vein as Whyne's canvasses, there is a sensuality and lushness expressed both in the subject matter and paint treatment. In

Mysteries — New Orleans, for instance, romantic elements such as swamps, pirates and Mardia Gras, are rendered in thickly applied paint with an expressionistic surface crudity. Both paintings by Boshier in this exhibition have an image of masked figures exposing their nakedness and sexually embracing with lust and passion. As many times occurs in Truman Capote's writings, there is a blending of the romantic, gothic element with sexuality.

Georgia-based artist Art Rosenbaum's paintings are populated with a combination of people and objects in an irrational clutter as in *Untitled* with an immobile and staring couple, a helmeted fireman, a grimacing woman frantically gesturing for protection, an elderly black woman slumped in a lawn chair. Expressing his own reactions to the impact of nuclear holocaust, the artist produces a surrealist space by the illogical placement of a high-rise apartment building, a large communications dish and a paved highway which ends abruptly with a sharp drop off, all in a flat, barren landscape with a fiery red sky. Rosenbaum's world with its political overtones and strong statements of social consciousness is not one of hope but of despair and resignation.

James Drake's *The Walk-in File Cabinet* is a full-size room, fabricated in steel, with seven pairs of doors — all closed. On each of the doors, labeled with such names as "cabinet of justice," "cards and arrows," or "knives and tears," is a symbol such as a snake, a black glove, a playing card, a black dog, each shaped in meticulous detail and proportion with multiple welded steel plates. Behind each door, hidden from the viewer, are largely autobiographical drawings. Through the sheer size and choice of images like the "suicide table" with its Derringer pistol, Christian cross and toy rocket accompanied by the "chair of inquisition," an uncanny ambiance is created. Similar to *The Lady or the Tiger*, Drake's sculptural environment is about choices — good and evil, right and wrong, and the storage of this information from life's experiences. Like his similar walk-in environment *Trophy Room* with its mounted taxidermied animals and overwhelming display of dangerous weapons, one senses the uncomfortable response of being consumed. In *The Walk-in File Cabinet*, with its commanding presence much like his Texas macho-ladden *Trophy Room*, Drake has created a personal mythology and private theatre which at the same time is universal.

The large-scale wall reliefs by Alexa Kleinbard are tableaux of figures acting and reacting. In *Spinning Wheel*, the tree branches become threatening tenacles reaching out to grab the group they surround. This element of fear, a common theme in her work, is absent from *On Your Mark, Get Ready*, another narrative relief of sports figures tumbling, juggling, weightlifting, fencing and sprinting.

Jimmy Jalapeeno is, as well as a painter, a performance artist whose "other" name, James N. Bonar, does not have the same theatricality and Texas "flavor." In the two oils presented here

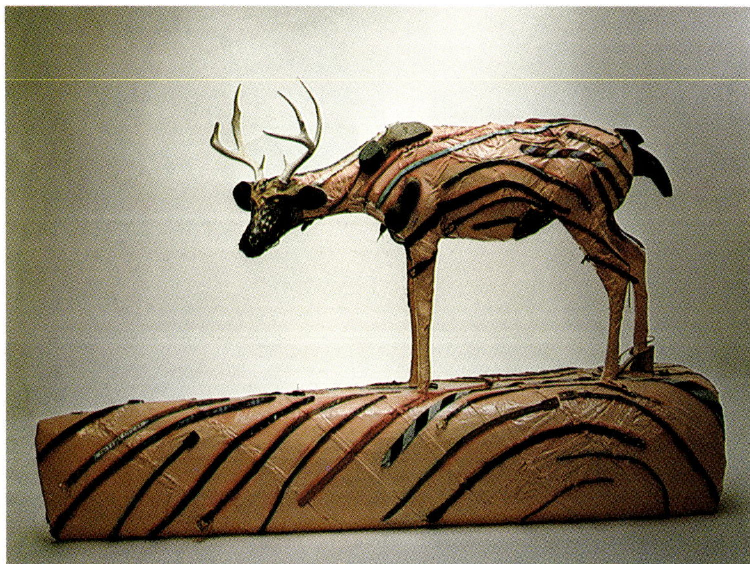

Ken Dawson Little

Shave 1983
Mixed media
58 × 90 × 31"
Courtesy the artist

costumed figures, as if characters in a play, perform on a stage-like setting. The use of crumpled drapery and a strong light source, whether in these "stage dramas" or in another series of works, plaster casts of classical sculpture, is evident for dramatic effect. A surrealistic private iconography manifests itself through-out the work. Illogical groupings of disparate personages pose in undefined relationships. There is an ambiguity of gesture (are the figures lolling about on the sofa or are they victims of violence?) and an obscurity of perception (is the brick-wall pattern part of the cast shadows or is it simply a product of being washed out by the strong light?). Even the confusion of the artist's name and the title of the paintings reinforces this irrational sensibility.

Without the obvious theatricality and highly formal stances found in Jalapeeno's paintings, the gouaches of Francie Rich are con-cerned with people — mainly blacks, lower middle-class whites such as the perpetual haircurler double-knit pants-suit set, the British royal family, American celebrities — presented with the snapshot quality of frozen and unnatural staged poses. Social gatherings such as women's tea parties, weddings, honky-tonk nightclubbing or informal group portraits are treated with a gentle mocking humor. Often, the titles she gives her works add to the narrative caricature and often suggest minor social mis-haps in a less than perfect environment, as found in Eudora Welty's stories and novels.

Like Rich's many of the subjects chosen by David Bates depict clichéd leisure activities of today's middle-class America — backyard barbecue, man and his dog, canoeing, trick or treating at Halloween or costuming for Mardi Gras. Unlike Rich's work there is an undercurrent of the sinister behind this facade of domestic bliss in Bates' large-scale canvasses, particularly in the pictures with the everpresent gloating smiles on masks. On both festive occasions one dresses for the purpose of losing or falsify-ing one's true identity to create a world of artificiality and give one license to behave in an abnormal and unrestricted manner. In his largely anecdotal and autobiographical pictures, Bates paints in a consciously naive style, reminiscent of the work of Southern black folk artists which he admires and collects. *The Sculptor* is the artist's tribute to the late folk sculptor William Edmondson of Nashville, whose work had a great influence on Bates.

Lee N. Smith III's combination painting/constructions are based on childhood experiences gathered while growing up in the outskirts of north Dallas. Recalling specific incidents while playing with friends in the wide open fields next to his family's house, Smith's narrative dreamscapes present an otherworldly milieu populated by mutant children with odd colored fleshtones, identical short haircuts and the staring eyes of sci-fi movies and comic books. Wearing simple, uniform clothing these child zom-bies participate in some kind of secret cult ceremonies with nightmarish associations. A single light source producing a cold eerie glow augments this surreal universe.

This macabre milieu is taken further in Russell Warren's *Not Knowing Who's Who* with the already impersonal sticklike figures hidden behind leering masks, generating a feeling of discomfort and impending danger. In *Parade* the identity of the figures is hidden behind the torch light held in the hands of the participants. Tension is heightened by surrealistic shadows stretching from far distances and the nervous, expressionistic application of paint with quick, short cross-hatch brushstrokes. Warren's work is characterized by personal myth to produce haunting ghost stories in the best Southern narrative, literary tradition.

The paintings of Earl Staley, a former teacher of Warren, depict invented private myths full of magic and fantasy as well as themes from the Bible and classical mythology. The curious marriage of classical themes presented with a highly emotional, romantic fervor mark the artist's unique treatment of antithetical attitudes. Working for the past couple of years at the American Academy in Rome, Staley's *An Enquentro* illustrates costumed figures, in tunics and helmets carrying spears and shields remi-niscent of the ancients, in a stagelike setting, suggestive of romantic Italian grand opera. Like the artist, the South in general, particularly during the antebellum era, has had a fascination with the ancient classical world, and its people have attempted to re-create and interpret its style of living. In this large painting, one senses a feeling of confrontation between these "Roman sol-diers" and unidentified black-hooded worshippers in procession with their canopied large idol. The painting combines classical elements with a representation of a Mexican religious ceremony. The artist often visits Mexico and retains strong emotional ties to that country, its customs and people. The theatrically charged exaggeration is heightened by a strong light source casting large, dramatic shadows on the participants in this imaginary dramatic scene of sorcery and ritual incantations. Similarly, in *The Triumph of Bacchus* Staley presents the incongruous coupling of the Roman myth of feasting and revelry set in a Mexican or Texas Big Bend landscape. In much the same way, Faulkner blends mytho-logical patterns and illusions in his stories of rural Mississippi — in *The Hamlet,* for example.

A few years ago Melissa Miller's paintings were largely autobio-graphical, recalling specific incidents and experiences as a youngster, many with tragic overtones, on her grandfather's Texas ranch. Always concerned with animals of all sorts, the farmyard fauna of the earlier work was sometimes only a threat, but now the beasts as in George Orwell's *Animal Farm* have taken over! Painted with an increasingly agitated surface and more intense palette, the once innocent monkeys, rabbits, and frogs now perform secret ritual dances on stilts. These humanoid creatures have lost all their innocence and now aggressively create their own world. The nervous energy of the handling of the paint coupled with the narrative action gives Miller's works an electrical charge full of drama and high emotion.

Similarly John Alexander has been painting large landscapes for some time, using quick, jittery notations which, when combined, form lyrical compositions with an anxious edge. The lack of a horizon line creates a tension and forces the viewer to become immersed into the picture. These expressionistic devices are enhanced by the addition of weird animallike forms peering through and haunting the space. One senses a feeling of uneasiness from flowers which threaten to become creatures and vice versa, recalling Odilon Redon's innocent-looking flower arrangements in which vermin and menacing insects seem to be lurking and hiding. In these works one experiences a less-natural environment and a more inherently dangerous world of fantasy and imagination. Tennessee Williams has often used such threatening flora and fauna images — consider *Suddenly Last Summer* with its man-eating plants and stories about Sebastian and Violet's visit to the Encantadas.

In the past two or three years, Robert Gordy has dramatically changed both his style and medium. In the late 1960s and continuing through the 1970s, he developed cool, highly stylized figures and environments with calculated and crisp delineation of forms in acrylic on canvas. Recently, Gordy has recycled a recurrent theme of monumental male heads in a less formalist manner reminiscent of his earlier 1960s drawing using bold and agitated gestures. Grotesque and grimacing, these tormented and tortured faces are executed in monoprint, a graphic technique which lends itself to spontaneity. Devoid of any anecdotal quality these visages, while retaining the character of individualized portraits, describe an angst and futility not seen with such intensity in Gordy's work of the 1970s.

Gael Stack's dark canvasses have a layering of graffitilike naive figures, words and symbols scribbled and scratched on a mottled field in a seemingly random and accidental manner. This gradual buildup of information over a period of time suggests a surface vandalized and mutilated while the notational, narrative quality becomes extremely personal and charged with emotion. Stack's art is about communication of feelings and ideas.

Richard Stout, who teaches at the University of Houston, also maintains a studio in Germany where he has exhibited repeatedly in both East and West. His painting reflects his interest in and admiration of the early twentieth-century German Expressionists. Loosely, thinly painted with sweeping motions of the brush, pairs of anonymous figures inhabit neutral environments in Stout's large canvasses such as *Brothers* and *The Breath of History #2*. The towering monumentality of these angst-ridden gesturing nudes is exaggerated by a perspective below center, from the level of the attenuated legs. The titles have broad sociological significance conveying the artist's concerns with expressing aspects of the human condition.

While the legacy of the Germans, particularly German Expressionism, is detectable in Stout's work, it is also common in concerns addressed for some time by Southern artists generally. One also recognizes this interest in the works of one of Stout's and Alexander's students in Houston, Julian Schnabel, who currently lives in New York City. The two works in the exhibition proclaim his firm sense of the past and of tradition. In one, *Family Tree*, the Southern notion of extended families is graphically recalled by a structure resembling that of genealogical charts, while in the other Schnabel exploits portraiture to remember his good friend and fellow artist Michael Tracy, a Texan. The artist's romantic, sentimental treatment of the subject is given an expressionistic handling with characteristic theatrical exaggeration, applying thick paint, broken plates and bondo to wood. Schnabel's art suggests reminiscences of personal experiences, attitudes about things, states of mind.

Rebecca Davenport's two still-life interiors *Mr. Harris* and *Sands Motel* are in fact another type of portraiture from the physiognomical representation painted by Schnabel. The general theme has a particular Southern legacy, and Davenport through her suggestive titles and elimination of figures gives it a new variation. The objects in these interiors possess a surreal character taking on a personification of their own by replacing figures. Through the clear suggestion and evidence of specific prior activity, one can apprehend the personality of the subject just as easily as if the artist had rendered a physical likeness.

Alabama-born William Christenberry's sculpture and his photographs are about the South — its people, its places, its history, its attitudes — engendering high emotional response. To a large extent it is a private art; one senses the feeling of being a voyeur when confronting the work, such as his Ku Klux Klan room environment which he has allowed to be viewed publicly only in recent years. Like the powerful sense of the past and of tradition evinced in Schnabel's work, Christenberry addresses, in the three pieces in this exhibition, another Southern predilection: a strong sense of place. The poignancy and sadness generated by so many deaths at Shiloh Battleground has captured not only his interest but that of other photographers working in the South, such as William Eggleston. In his carefully researched works, Christenberry has created a series of monumental sculptures to the Southern experience incorporating materials indigenous to the rural landscape such as Alabama red soil and rusted tin as often seen in old metal advertisement signs, like Flannery O'Connor's attention to local details of her Georgia setting.

Like the photographs of Christenberry, the images in this exhibition by William Eggleston from Memphis focus on a Southern monument and specific location: Graceland, Elvis Presley's lavish mansion. Both sites, Graceland and Shiloh, serve as memorials to two types of dead heroes, and Christenberry and Eggleston as ''Southern boys'' honor and pay tribute to their ancestral heritage — a Southern duty. The color photographs by Eggleston, who has devoted his life's work to describing life in the South, present a classic definition of the romantic viewpoint: a subordination of form to content, emphasis on emotion and introspection, and a celebration of the common man and freedom of the spirit.

The romantic universe of James Surls is filled with dreams and visions. This highly personal fantasy world of wood sculpture, drawings, and poetry has clear references to the land and displays a genuine love of nature. Surls' art has a strong sense of place and tradition and his sculptures often have a feeling of becoming totemic monuments to these belief systems. His carving can be associated with black folk artists' predilection for whittling walking sticks and children's toys. It is a rural art stemming from the craft of woodworking but executed with a firm understanding and feeling for art history and the sculptural tradition. In works like *Me, the Axe, the Wand* Surls unravels fantastic myths incorporating himself and invented creatures, not without a bit of tongue-in-cheek humor and exaggeration.

The ritualistic shrines and fetishes created by Roy Fridge out of materials found in nature — wood, bones, antlers — speak to undefined spirit cults and pagan religions of primitive cultures. Even though *Bone Boat in the Branches* and *Standing Shaman Shrine* are elegant in themselves, their heritage is informed by a folk art tradition emcompassing a basic simplicity and the honesty of relatively unsophisticated peoples. Fridge's anthropologically derived sculptures evoke a powerful presence and an emotional response of private visions, dreams and belief systems. They conjure romantic and theatrical notions of the unknown. These totems and reliquaries of the imagination, even

though personal, have a universal appeal and identification. One is reminded of James Dickey's well-known poem "Sheep Child" in which Georgia boys frighten themselves with stories of an alleged creature, half human, half sheep kept in a jar in a museum in Atlanta.

Ken Dawson Little's primary concerns are expression and communication through totemic or iconic representations, sometimes painted, sometimes with applied commonplace found objects such as broken dishes and pottery shards or, more recently, clothes and foot apparel — leather shoes, boots, sneakers — creating a highly sensuous and tactile surface. These sculptured assemblages incorporating unconventional materials, undisguised from their normal intended usage give the work an honesty and directness often found in naive folk art. This physicality recalls figures from the Cameroons in Africa (seen by Little in an art museum) which are completely covered from head to foot with either small glass beads or cowrie shells. Two favorite themes, boats and animals, act as symbols for particular narrative or expressive ideas, all explicitly personal and autobiographical, often combining the feelings of poignance and humor in a single piece. For example, the amusing and ingenious utilization of the applied materials is coupled with the notion of violence and death suggested by the motif of taxidermied animal trophies. There is a pathos and irony in the shoe leather being recycled to become, once again, animal skin but in a new context, as in *Fury*. Little's predilection for making portraits of close friends and relatives reinforces this notion of a highly individualized subject matter with strong surrealist overtones through the odd juxtaposition of unrelated materials and subjects in a single unit.

For the most part, Southern artists ignored the lead of the popular movements of the 1960s and 1970s — Pop, Op, Minimal. There was, and continues to be, no genuine interest in strict formalist concerns. On the other hand black folk art references crop up with frequency. As has been demonstrated in this exhibition, the art of the South, and its culture in general, is more emotionally based and less cerebral than that of these artists' counterparts in other parts of the country, particularly on the East Coast. The incidence of good non-objective, abstract painting being done in the South is limited while figurative styles have predominated for some time. The strong literary, narrative tradition lends itself to an art drawing upon personal experience with autobiographical references prevalent. With a basic response to one's environment this predilection toward sensitive introspection is illustrated through stylistic idioms identified with emotional content. There is an expressionistic quality in which forms are distorted or exaggerated and colors intensified. The romantic emphasis of imagination and fantasy and the surrealist tendencies toward the irrational and the subconscious proliferates. These characteristics applied individually or collectively present a diverse body of work which is indicative of and, in many ways, peculiar to the culture and consciousness of the Southern region.

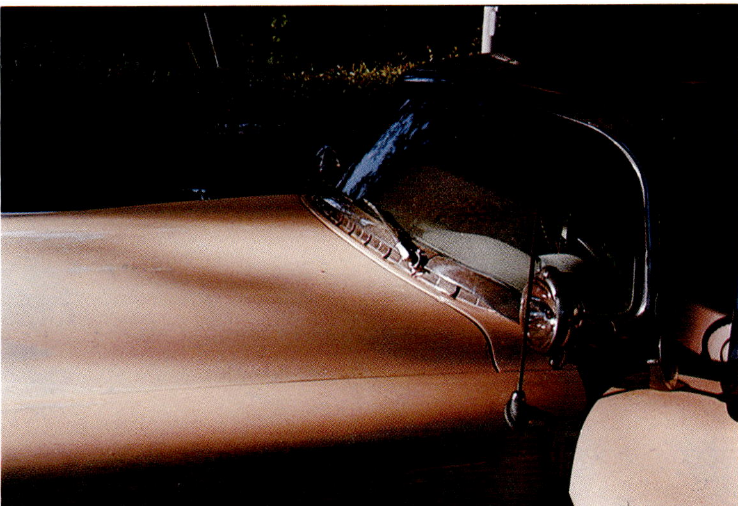

William Eggleston

Graceland 1983
Dye-transfer print
20 × 24"
Courtesy the artist and
Middendorf Gallery, Washington, D.C.

Southern Fictions by Dr. Monroe K. Spears

These works are Southern fictions in the literal sense since they are works made by Southerners. The title suggests also, however, that there is a resemblance between these works and Southern prose fiction — the novels and stories of William Faulkner, Eudora Welty, Flannery O'Connor and later writers. The Southern quality shared by these prose and art works is real and important, though to define it in a few pages is a difficult assignment comparable to inscribing the Gettysburg Address on the head of a pin. (W. J. Cash, in what is still the best book on the subject — *The Mind of the South* — required well over four hundred pages.)

If patriotism is the last refuge of a scoundrel, as Dr. Johnson said, then regionalism is surely the first refuge of the pretentious untalented, of those provincials who want to be big frogs in little puddles. Yet regionalism is inescapable. Like it or not, we must come from somewhere and exist in one place rather than another; and awareness of places is an essential part of self-knowledge. Place and time are two coordinates that define our existence, so to speak, and to know who we are is to understand the point at which they intersect. Only through this self-knowledge can the artist achieve authenticity and truth to personal experience.

Bad art (unless technically incompetent) is usually an imitation of art of another time and place; bad American art has usually imitated European art of the recent past. Regionalism is obviously no virtue in itself. While it is never an excuse or justification, it is a necessary part of the artist's vision. As Max Apple said in the introduction to his anthology, *Southwestern Fiction,* "There are no boundaries to regionalism; when you see the Southwest you are seeing everything. The local language and customs, the small matters that separate us, these things, properly noticed, become the bond that unites us."

Regional awareness may manifest itself as hate as well as love and is in fact usually ambivalent. A classic example is Faulkner's *Absalom, Absalom!,* in which Quentin, asked at the end why he hates the South, replies "quickly, at once immediately; 'I dont hate it,' he said. *I dont hate it* he thought, panting in the cold air, the iron New England dark; *I dont. I dont! I dont hate it! I dont hate it!*" An equally impressive and paradoxical example is James Joyce, who would have nothing to do with the Irish Renaissance, detested literary patriots and professional Gaels, exiled himself from Ireland but then spent the rest of his life writing obsessively about Dublin.

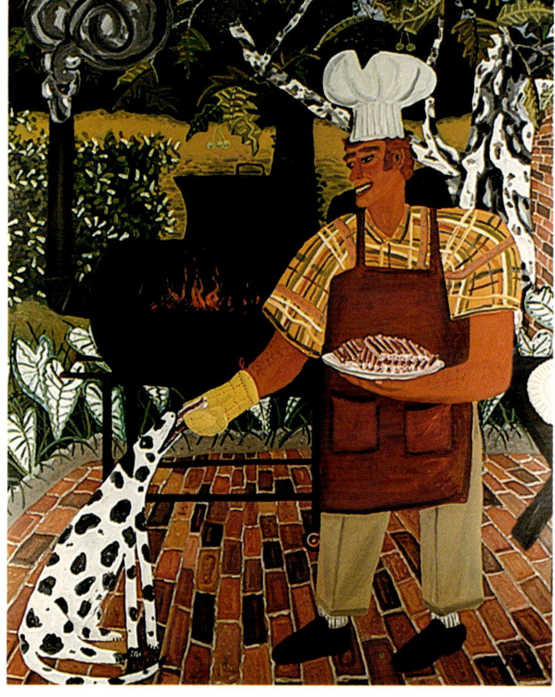

David Bates

Backyard Bar-B-Q 1982
Oil on canvas
96 × 78"
Courtesy the artist and
Charles Cowles Gallery, New York City

Conceding, perhaps reluctantly, that regionalism is inescapable and important, we may yet wonder whether the South still exists as a meaningful region. Perhaps the South itself has now become a Southern Fiction. In the largest cities, the population is highly mobile, cosmopolitan and often transient. Here, especially in speaking of visual artists, who, in order to obtain instruction and recognition, must be in touch with artists, teachers, critics and dealers in the major art capitals of the world, it must be admitted that doubts do arise.

There are obviously many Souths, or many sub-regions of the South. For example, cattle and cowboys and oil and chemicals have made Texas more Southwestern than the rest of the Confederacy in some respects. All superficial regional differences in speech, dress, customs, manners and the like have been steadily eroding for a long time under the accelerating pressures of the mass media (TV most of all) and of the advertisers and franchise chains who have made all America look the same. Yet I should venture to assert that the South does still exist and that Texas is still part of it.

There are, I believe, distinctively Southern qualities that are characteristic of most people throughout the region and that are clearly recognizable in the art they produce. (Of course, these are not absolute distinctions, but matters of degree and emphasis, for Southerners are not completely different from everyone else.) Let me suggest two such qualities that seem relevant to this exhibition. In the first place, Southerners tend to be more humane

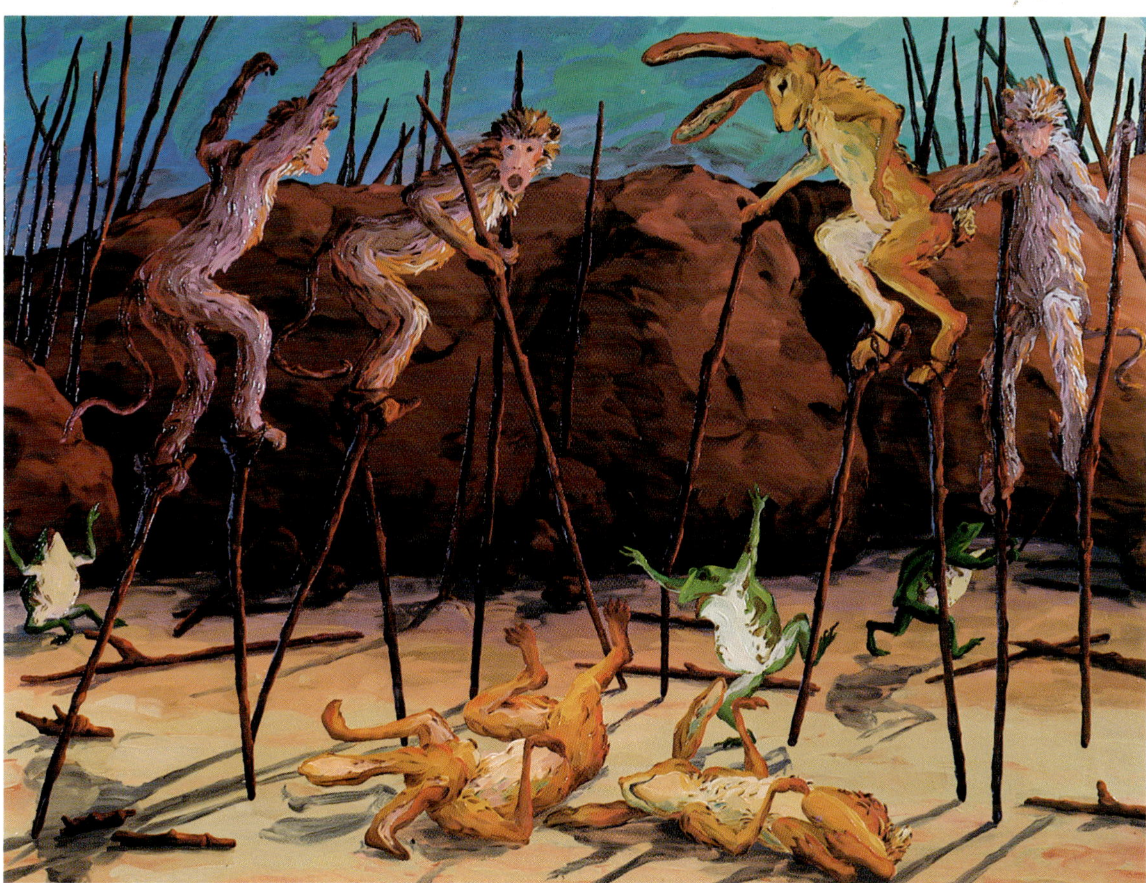

Melissa Miller

Clowns 1983
Oil on canvas
56 × 76"
Collection Mr. and Mrs. I. H. Kempner III,
Houston, Texas

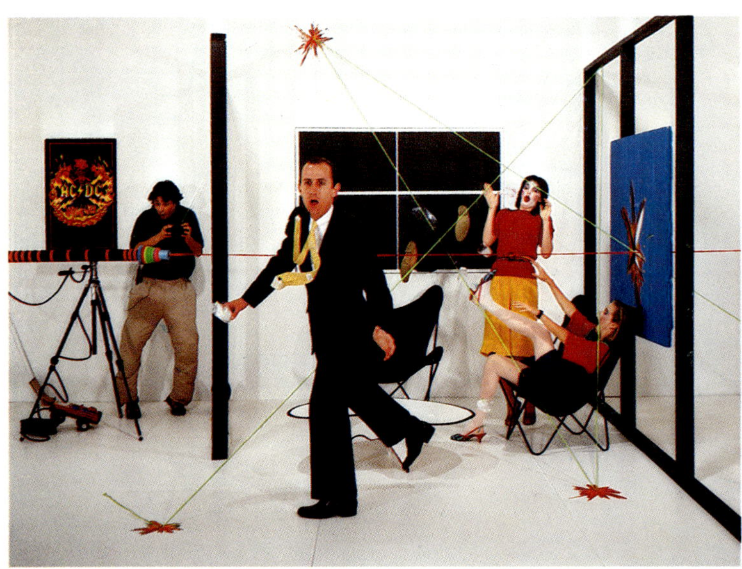

Nic Nicosia

Near Modern Disaster #2 1983
Cibachrome print
40 × 50"
Courtesy the artist and Delahunty Gallery,
Dallas, Texas

than people in the other regions. They are human — sometimes all too human. Traditionally, they give human relations priority over all other values: family most of all, extending to the farthest boundaries of kinship, but also hospitality to the stranger and an immense variety of relationships in between. This implicit value is expressed in the warmth, ease and courtesy of Southern manners at their best and in the effort made to amuse and entertain. This quality of thoughtfulness, sympathy and compassion derives not from aristocratic lineage (real or imaginary) but from a shared heritage of guilt, suffering and tragedy in the Civil War and its long aftermath. Southerners are more aware of their ancestors, of tradition and of the burden of the past than are most other people. And what this makes them realize (except for the occasional few who, like Faulkner's Hightower, are imprisoned in the past) is their common humanity. Since they have known evil and defeat, Southerners do not expect innocence, automatic progress or absolute righteousness, either for themselves or their country. Southerners still profess high ideals and a more demanding code of personal honor than others, but these high professions are balanced by a constant awareness that, as John Henry said to the Captain, "A man ain't nuthin but a man."

The second quality I would propose as distinctively Southern is a propensity for creating and believing fictions — anecdotes, stories, legends, myths — about themselves. These fictions are not lies in the sense of being deliberately contrary to fact; they contain at least a kernel of truth; but they are imaginative constructions ranging in motive from the teasing humor of the tall tale to the desire to escape unpleasant reality. For obvious examples, there are the myths that the Old South was populated exclusively by ladies and gentlemen descended from aristocratic Cavaliers, following as closely as possible the manners of medieval chivalry as depicted by Sir Walter Scott and living on large plantations manned by slaves who loved their masters and were happy in their servitude. Many of these myths were nostalgic and defensive back-projections from the hard times of Reconstruction and after, but the basic myths were believed by many antebellum Southerners, who often tried to embody them in real life.

To distinguish myth from reality has been a central preoccupation of Southern artists since antebellum days. *The White Rose of Memphis,* by William Faulkner's great-grandfather, Col. W. C. Faulkner, is an early example. Throughout the book, the romantic and chivalric doings on board the steamboat are counterpointed by the realistic episodes on the river banks. Faulkner himself constantly explores the meaning of the myths and legends of the South and their relation to reality. In Robert Penn Warren's *All the King's Men,* Jack Burden slowly and painfully discovers the truth about Willie Stark, about his own fathers and about himself. Katherine Anne Porter's great story "Old Mortality" deals with the protagonist's long effort to find out the truth about the romantic legend of the Southern belle Amy and apply the lessons learned to her own life. Southern historians, too, have found a rich field not in simply "debunking" the myths but in studying the complex interactions of myth and reality in the South. In addition to W. J. Cash's *Mind of the South* and C. Vann Woodward's *Burden of Southern History,* a brilliant new book by Bertram Wyatt-Brown, *Southern Honor,* provides an excellent example.

The South of John Crowe Ransom's beautiful poem "Antique Harvesters" — "the Proud Lady, of the heart of fire, The look of snow," who does not age, and who is served gladly, without hope of reward, by chivalric young men, is a central symbol of the imaginary land where all men are honorable and all ladies virtuous. The Southern woman, says Cash, "was the lily-pure maid of Astolat and the hunting goddess of the Boeotian hill. And — she was the pitiful Mother of God. Merely to mention her was to send strong men into tears — or shouts."

Such myths have been used to manipulate the South from very early times. I remember myself that great demagogue Cotton Ed Smith, who in my youth was rounding out a very long career in the U.S. Senate based on an unvarying platform of States' Rights, White Supremacy and the Purity of Southern Womanhood. It would be hard to say now which part of this famous trinity is more completely obsolete — or which part the South was most relieved to get rid of. It was not only Southerners who were victims of such stereotypes, but Northerners, too.

When I left my native South Carolina for my first extended stay in the North, at Princeton, I made friends with a boy from Minneapolis who promptly assured me that Southerners knew how to manage horses and women, and therefore he was counting on me for guidance. No doubt he saw me as the archetypal slave-owner, putting horses and women (black) through their paces and firmly in command. As a middle-class small-town Southerner, I had little experience and less assurance in dealing with either horses or women; but I let him keep his illusions.

If I am right in suggesting that a special susceptibility to illusion and myth about itself has always been characteristic of the South, and that its historians and literary artists have been preoccupied with the exposure of self-deception and the discrimination of myth from reality in recent years, the next question is whether the same preoccupation is apparent in the works of the visual artists here exhibited. In the first place, twelve of them are primarily workers in collage or related forms — assemblages, combines, installations — rather than in painting or sculpture in

the traditional sense. Certainly one aim of collage is to break down the distinction between the world of illusion and the world of reality by bringing real objects into the art world. The viewer is to be prevented from making a safe and comfortable separation between art and reality, as the audiences of modern plays and novels are prevented from escaping into a more beautiful and comprehensible world of illusion. Even photography is used in ingenious ways by these artists to break down the barrier between art and reality. Fiction is thus revealed as fiction, while at the same time the aesthetic qualities of ordinary objects and materials are revealed in a new way.

I am not saying that all collage has the intentions I have suggested; the subject is far too complex for such generalization. If all collage is in a sense abstract, it is also in a sense narrative both of the history of the materials and of the artist's process of working. Much of it is also funny through deliberate incongruity; much of it incorporates elements of folk-naive and popular art. Perhaps it is worth noting that two of the leading recent collagists, Robert Rauschenberg and Jasper Johns, were born and raised in the South, though they are no longer Southerners in the same sense as those exhibited here — that is, artists now identified with the South.

As to humaneness, the other basic quality I have ascribed to the South, the present exhibition is part of a large movement in the visual arts that may be called rehumanization. As Charmaine Locke, a Houston artist, said in the foreword to the catalogue which accompanied an exhibition called *Images of the House,* "We are seeing a return to humanistic issues, a re-evaluation of the personal, the experiential, as sources for art...." The same trend is apparent in the *1983 New Orleans Triennial,* as it was in the two preceding ones. While this movement is certainly not peculiar to the South, it would seem to be even stronger and older here than elsewhere, and it takes certain distinctive forms which this exhibition undertakes to reveal.

Rehumanization represents for many artists a shift from the Minimalist and Conceptualist art which has dominated the recent mainstream art, to the personal and the human. A revival of figuration is central to this interest but abstraction is not excluded (for example, some swampy paintings by John Alexander). Most of the New York and European artists working in this manner have been called Neo-Expressionists or Figurative Expressionists but a significant and lively tradition of humanistic and expressionistic art has prevailed in this region for some time.

As far as formal media are concerned, the deliberate breakdown of distinctions continues for these artists as well as those working in other regions. The viewer can't tell painting from photography from sculpture (which may be hard as welded metal, as in James Drake's installations, or soft as draped fabric in Donald Beason's) or any of these from the pieces of reality with which they are combined. (There are, of course, some thoroughly traditional paintings and sculptures.) But of formalism in the sense of impersonal detachment there is none. These works are highly expressive of emotion and are in this sense expressionist. Art Rosenbaum is a striking example. (Many of them display a direct relation to German Expressionism — for example, those of Richard Stout.) Many of these works are very personal and openly autobiographical, drawn without disguise from the artist's own life. Even those works with an obvious mythological or archetypal motif are often described by the artist in personal terms. Several of the works deal with domestic scenes, with both the interior of the house and with the family, in which the artists do not hesitate to include themselves.

The Southern preoccupation with fiction is more obviously apparent in these works than in collage. Many of the works are anecdotal or narrative in that they tell or imply stories. (For example, Alexa Kleinbard's large wall reliefs with their gestural figures.) This is itself a humane quality, and no more exclusively Southern than love of family: as Sir Philip Sidney long ago observed, a good story can hold children from play and old men from the chimney corner. But Southerners traditionally like them even more than other people. They spend more time telling them and listening to them, and as Southern orators have always known, they are more likely to be convinced by a story than by an abstract argument. The Old South was perhaps more influenced by art than any other society in history, though unfortunately the art was not of very high quality and was confused with history. Southerners, when they were not pretending to be Periclean Greeks or Romans of the Republic, were attempting to imitate in real life the fake medieval world of Sir Walter Scott's novels, complete with names, manners, costumes and tournaments.

Their passion for Greek Revival architecture, for high-flown rhetoric and for imaginary genealogy has not yet disappeared, though the "best people" are no longer referred to as "the chivalry" and there is some awareness that even the Old South was dominated by the frontier rather than by aristocratic planters.

But Southerners, "the most sentimental people in history," have always been easily self-deceived. While not valuing art for its own sake, they have always been too ready to take fiction for fact. Hence they have needed help from their artists in distinguishing the two. From Mark Twain, whose account in *Huckleberry Finn* of the funereal art of Miss Emmeline Grangerford and of the feud is a devastatingly comic picture of the real Old South, to Tennessee Williams with his pathetic and terrifying Southern ladies, they have received it. Since narrative has been out of fashion in painting since the sentimental "literary" painting of the pre-Raphaelites, to reinject a narrative element into the art is to recover a lost domain.

Many of these works are funny, such as Ken Dawson Little's sculptures of pigs made out of old shoes. Yet, the humor is more often grotesque and grim, intended more to disturb than to amuse, witness Julian Schnabel's collages made of broken plates, Melissa Miller's "dramas that play when our backs are turned" and most of Nic Nicosia's domestic dramas, staged and photographed.

There is a strong apocalyptic vein in many of these works, a sense of doom and foreboding, of waiting for something dreadful to happen. This theme contrasts with the images of domesticity, which feel in danger of being imperilled or destroyed. The human form is often shown as distorted, made into a mannikin or mummylike figure or modeling-armature (Donald Beason) — in short, dehumanized. Awareness and horror of this fearsome possibility of loss of humanity are, of course, far more peculiar to the South; but are perhaps stronger here than in other regions. Consider, for literary analogies, the novels of Walker Percy, especially *Love in the Ruins* and *The Second Coming*; or the poems of James Dickey, such as "May-Day Sermon," "The Fire-Bombing" or *The Zodiac.* No doubt this tendency is related to the fundamentalist and revivalist religion that is prevalent in the South, with its doomsday terrors and fire and brimstone rhetoric. But it is also true to say that since the South has been more aware of the importance of human values, of the relation of the individual to family, domestic life and community rather than his problems in isolation, it is natural that the Southern artist should be even more sensitive than others to the threats to these values implicit in our contemporary world.

It is noteworthy that, though many of these works are by implication strongly critical of our civilization, there are none that are in any sense propagandistic or programmatically political. One reason that the Old South lacked much serious interest in the arts is that its best intellectual energies went into politics and that its commitment to slavery imposed a political orthodoxy on artists that obviously was severely limiting to them. The artists here represented are plainly not limited by adherence to any political orthodoxy or unorthodoxy; they are aware socially but not in terms of political abstractions. But their South is very different from the South of stereotype, myth, legend and fictions in general. The world of minorities is represented, but an important subject is what used to be called the poor white. The poor white is seen not as stereotype — neither the white trash caricatured by Erskine Caldwell nor the hillbilly — but as ordinary Americans; and so are the minorities. We have had this kind of treatment in literature for some years. From good early treatment of blacks by such white writers as DuBose Heyward and Julia Peterkin we have moved to such fine black writers as Ralph Ellison, James Baldwin, Al Young and Alice Walker. Indian writers such as N. Scott Momaday and Leslie Silko have dealt with their own race. William Price Fox in *Southern Fried* and *Ruby Red* deals with poor white South Carolinians and the country music scene, as does C. W. Smith in Texas, with his *Country Music* and Beverly Lowry with *Daddy's Girl.* It is amusing to reflect that Nashville was once the Athens of the South, noted mainly for its educational distinction, symbolized in its replica of the Parthenon, and its location as the headquarters of the Fugitive-Agrarians, with their defense of what they took to be the lasting values of the Old South. Now Nashville is the home of the Nashville Sound, the capital of country music. In strange conjunction one can still see *Hee-Haw* and the Lost Cause, the old classical-chivalric ideals and Opryland; though there is little doubt which side has the power and the future.

There is much fantasy in this exhibition and a strong surrealist element, though not the fantastic realism of René Magritte, Paul Delvaux, Salvador Dali and the like. The use of surrealistic images is much closer to the folk and the comic, sometimes even the comics and pop. The folk-naive and Neo-Primitive strains are also powerful. For example, David Bates with his *Backyard Bar-B-Q* or Francie Rich with her portrait of *Couple.* Works like Lee N. Smith III's *Breaking the Ice* relate to this folk tradition, but are also highly emotional, directly related to personal experience, fantastic but also narrative and direct. Susan Whyne and Jimmy Jalapeeno combine the folk tradition with classical techniques and allusions in a fascinating manner, as in Jalapeeno's *March 25th, #1* or Whyne's *Flamenco and the Nic-Nac Man*, which is both fantastic and emotional, somewhat in the manner of Marc Chagall.

It is tempting to draw further parallels between these artists and other modern Southern writers, in addition to those already mentioned. Flannery O'Connor's grimly humorous satiric realism which shades into the grotesque and fantastic is suggested by many of these works (perhaps especially those of Melissa Miller and Russell Warren), and so are aspects of Donald Barthelme, William Goyen and that converted Southerner Max Apple, who are in their very different ways comic and fantastic writers. Larry McMurtry, who used to wear a T-shirt labeled "Minor Regional Novelist," is like them in his scrupulous recording of the regional scene as well as in his frequent use of the comic-grotesque tone. And that greatest of all regional artists, William Faulkner (though one must immediately say, greatest with the possible exception of Yeats, and must note that it might be better to call them both the most regional of great artists rather than the other way around), provides innumerable similarities in his rendering of life at once Southern and universal.

No writer could be a better example of the humaneness and the special concern with distinguishing fiction from fact — or better, with discerning the truth that lies in fiction, legend, myth and stories of all kinds — than Faulkner. How things and people look in one place rather than another was as important to Faulkner as to any visual artist, and yet he was very clear that this regional aspect was not as important as the universal. The title of *Light in August,* he said, was intended to suggest a special quality of the light in Mississippi when about the middle of August "suddenly there's a foretaste of fall, it's cool, there's a lambence, a luminous quality to the light. . . ." But that luminosity, he continues, is "older than our Christian civilization"; it seems to come from "back in the old classic times . . . from Greece, from Olympus." Though he doesn't say so, he is obviously thinking of Greek tragedy, in which the human condition was similarly portrayed in terms both local and universal. The Southern fictions of this show, like Faulkner's, strive to become fictions that are true and universal as well as Southern.

Catalogue of the Exhibition

All dimensions are given in inches, height preceding width, preceding depth.

John Alexander

Untitled 1981
Oil on canvas
48 × 48″
Courtesy the artist and
Janie C. Lee Gallery,
Houston, Texas

Flora, Fauna and Family Affairs 1982
Oil on canvas
78 × 84″
Collection Joanna Rogers, Dallas, Texas

David Bates

Backyard Bar-B-Q 1982
Oil on canvas
96 × 78″
Courtesy the artist and
Charles Cowles Gallery, New York City

The Sculptor 1983
Oil on canvas
78 × 96″
Courtesy the artist and
Charles Cowles Gallery, New York City

Donald Beason

Houston — Midnight 1983
Mixed media
Triangular area: each side, 288 × 288 × 228″
Courtesy the artist

Derek Boshier

Ku Klux Klan 1982
Oil on canvas
84 × 48″
Courtesy the artist and
Texas Gallery, Houston

Mysteries — New Orleans 1983
Oil on canvas
88¹/₂ × 134″
Courtesy the artist and
Texas Gallery, Houston

William Christenberry

Bloody Pond, Shiloh Battlefield, Tennessee 1980
ECK 74 print
20 × 24″
Courtesy the artist and Middendorf
Gallery, Washington, D.C.

Sweeny Monument (View I), Shiloh Battlefield, Tennessee 1980
ECK 74 print
20 × 24″
Courtesy the artist and Middendorf
Gallery, Washington, D.C.

Southern Monument XII (Shiloh) 1982
Mixed media with Alabama red soil
6 × 17¹/₂ × 23″
Courtesy Moody Gallery, Houston, Texas

Rebecca Davenport

Mr. Harris 1979
Oil on canvas
72 × 96″
Collection Hanoj and Myrna Perez,
North Miami Beach, Florida

Sands Motel 1980
Oil on canvas
60 × 60″
Collection Renée Jacobs,
Morristown, New Jersey

James Drake

The Walk-in File Cabinet 1983
Welded steel and conti crayon
96 × 72 × 120″
Courtesy the artist

William Eggleston

Graceland 1983
Dye-transfer print
20 × 24″
Courtesy the artist and
Middendorf Gallery,
Washington, D.C.

Graceland 1983
Dye-transfer print
20 × 24"
Courtesy the artist and
Middendorf Gallery,
Washington, D.C.

Graceland 1983
Dye-transfer print
20 × 24"
Courtesy the artist and
Middendorf Gallery,
Washington, D.C.

Graceland 1983
Dye-transfer print
20 × 24"
Courtesy the artist and
Middendorf Gallery,
Washington, D.C.

Vernon Fisher

Snakes and Ladders 1982
Mixed media
135 × 59 × 6"
Collection Robert K. Hoffman, Dallas,
Texas

Tent Show 1983
Mixed media
Blackboard and chair: 56 × 61 × 20";
Acrylic on laminated paper: 72 × 93½"
Collection Dennis Bieber, Courtesy
Barbara Gladstone Gallery, New York City

Roy Fridge

Bone Boat in the Branches 1982
Wood and deer skull mask
73 × 26½ × 27"
Collection Mr. and Mrs. Richard C.
Roeder, Houston, Texas

Standing Shaman Shrine 1982
Wood, cloth and deer skull mask
108 × 30 × 14"
Courtesy the artist and Moody Gallery,
Houston, Texas

Robert Gordy

Study for "Quint" (1st version) 1982
Monoprint
19¾ × 15½"
Courtesy the artist

Male Head (3rd version) 1983
Monoprint
17⅝ × 13"
Courtesy the artist

Roman Head (4th version) 1983
Monoprint
26⅞ × 19⅝"
Courtesy the artist

Jimmy Jalapeeno

March 25th, #1 1983
Oil on canvas
60 × 84"
Courtesy the artist

March 25th, #8 1983
Oil on canvas
48 × 72"
Courtesy the artist

Alexa Kleinbard

On Your Mark, Get Ready 1982
Celluclay, rhoplex, screen, wood
and acrylic
60 × 156 × 8"
Courtesy the artist

Spinning Wheel 1982
Celluclay, rhoplex, screen, wood
and acrylic
72 × 102 × 16"
Courtesy the artist

Clarence John Laughlin

Possessed by the Past 1939
Gelatin silver print
13¾ × 10"
Collection Ian Glennie and Fredericka
Hunter, Houston, Texas

The Enigma 1941
Gelatin silver print
14 × 10¾"
Collection Helen and Rick Gardner,
Houston, Texas

The Repulsive Bed 1941
Gelatin silver print
15½ × 20"
Collection Martin Owen, Houston, Texas

The Unborn 1941
Gelatin silver print
13³/₄ × 10³/₄"
Collection Robin Cronin and John
Stephenson, Houston, Texas

The Unending Stream 1941
Gelatin silver print
10³/₄" × 13³/₄
Collection Robert E. Kinnaman and
Brian A. Ramaekers, Houston, Texas

Final Paradise for Dead Birds 1951
Gelatin silver print
14 × 17"
Collection Robin Cronin and John
Stephenson, Houston, Texas

Ken Dawson Little

Fury 1983
Mixed media
56 × 90 × 31"
Courtesy the artist

Shave 1983
Mixed media
58 × 90 × 31"
Courtesy the artist

Ed McGowin

Rescue 1983
Mixed media
120 × 144"
Courtesy the artist and Iolas/Jackson
Gallery, New York City

Robbery 1983
Mixed media
84 × 84"
Courtesy the artist and Iolas/Jackson
Gallery, New York City

Melissa Miller

Untitled (Tigers) 1982
Oil on canvas
58 × 70"
Collection Bob Wilson, Houston, Texas

Clowns 1983
Oil on canvas
56 × 76"
Collection Mr. and Mrs. I. H. Kempner III,
Houston, Texas

Nic Nicosia

*Domestic Drama #7 (Near Modern
Disaster #1)* 1982
Cibachrome print
40 × 50"
Collection Steve Dennie, Dallas, Texas

Near Modern Disaster #2 1983
Cibachrome print
40 × 50"
Courtesy the artist and Delahunty Gallery,
Dallas, Texas

Francie Rich

Used Car Salesman and His Daughters
1980-1982
Gouache on paper
13¹/₂ × 17"
Courtesy the artist

Good Size Negro Lady 1982
Gouache on paper
17¹/₄ × 13"
Courtesy the artist

The Convention 1983
Gouache on paper
14¹/₂ × 18"
Courtesy the artist

Couple 1983
Gouache on paper
17¹/₂ × 13¹/₂"
Courtesy the artist

Art Rosenbaum

Outside Carnesville 1983
Oil and alkyd resin on canvas
66 × 78"
Courtesy the artist

Untitled 1983
Oil and alkyd resin on canvas
60 × 64"
Courtesy the artist

Julian Schnabel

Family Tree 1982
Oil on wood
119¹/₂ × 70¹/₂"
Courtesy the artist

Portrait of Michael Tracy 1983
Oil, plates and bondo on wood
48 × 40″
Collection Michael Tracy,
San Ygnacio, Texas

Lee N. Smith III

Breaking the Ice 1983
Oil on canvas
66 × 99″
Collection Atlantic Richfield Company,
Dallas, Texas

In the Morning 1983
Oil on canvas
66 × 82″
Courtesy the artist and DW Gallery,
Dallas, Texas

Gael Stack

Call Maureen 1982
Mixed media on canvas
36³/₈ × 48¹/₄″
Collection Betty Moody, Houston, Texas

The Goodbye 1983
Mixed media on canvas
52¹/₄ × 80¹/₂″:
2 panels, each 52¹/₄ × 40¹/₄″
Courtesy the artist and Janie C. Lee
Gallery, Houston, Texas

Earl Staley

An Encuentro 1981
Acrylic on canvas
59³/₄ × 83³/₄″
Courtesy the artist and Watson/de Nagy
and Company, Houston, Texas

The Triumph of Bacchus 1982
Acrylic on canvas
51¹/₂ × 83¹/₂″
Courtesy the artist and Watson/de Nagy
and Company, Houston, Texas

Richard Stout

Brothers 1982
Acrylic on canvas
72 × 50″
Courtesy the artist and Meredith Long
and Company, Houston, Texas

The Breath of History #2 1983
Acrylic on canvas
72 × 50″
Courtesy the artist and Meredith Long
and Company, Houston, Texas

James Surls

*I Am Building with the Axe, the Knife,
and the Needle's Eye* 1982
Hickory, oak, pine, padouk and mahogany
160 × 67³/₄ × 49″
Collection The Museum of Fine Arts,
Houston; purchased with funds provided
by Texas Eastern Corporation

Me, the Axe, the Wand 1982
Pine, mahogany, oak, hickory and rattan
125¹/₂ × 44 × 26″
Courtesy the artist and Delahunty Gallery,
Dallas, Texas

Russell Warren

Not Knowing Who's Who 1983
Acrylic on canvas
60 × 55″
Courtesy the artist and
Phyllis Kind Gallery, New York City

Parade 1983
Acrylic on canvas
55 × 72″
Courtesy the artist and
Phyllis Kind Gallery, New York City

Susan Whyne

The Date 1983
Oil on canvas
90 × 65″
Courtesy the artist

Flamenco and the Nic-Nac Man 1983
Oil on canvas
90 × 65″
Courtesy the artist

John Alexander

1945
Born, Beaumont, Texas
1968
B.F.A., Lamar University, Beaumont, Texas
1970
M.F.A., Southern Methodist University,
Dallas, Texas

The artist was an assistant professor at
the University of Houston, Texas, from
1975 to 1980. He lives and works in
New York City.

Selected Solo Exhibitions

1975
Contemporary Arts Museum,
Houston, Texas
Meredith Long and Company,
Houston, Texas
1976
Kornblatt Gallery, Baltimore, Maryland
Meredith Long and Company,
Houston, Texas
1977
Delahunty Gallery, Dallas, Texas
Kornblatt Gallery, Baltimore, Maryland
Long Beach Museum of Art, California
1978
Max Hutchinson Gallery, New York City
1980
The Corcoran Gallery of Art,
Washington, D.C.
1981
Dobrick Gallery, Chicago, Illinois
1982
Diane Brown Gallery, Washington, D.C.
The Janie C. Lee Gallery, Houston, Texas
1983
Marlborough Gallery, New York City

Selected Group Exhibitions

1976
The American Academy and Institute of
Arts and Letters, New York City
*National Print and Drawing Annual
Exhibition,* Davidson College,
North Carolina
Philadelphia Houston Exchange, Institute
of Contemporary Art, University of
Pennsylvania, Philadelphia
Selections for New and Old Collections,
Art Museum of South Texas,
Corpus Christi

1977
1977 Artists Biennial, New Orleans
Museum of Art, Louisiana
19th Annual Eight State Exhibition,
Oklahoma Art Center, Oklahoma City
Six Painters Southwest, Museum of Art,
University of Oklahoma, Norman
*The 35th Biennial Exhibition of
Contemporary American Painting,* The
Corcoran Gallery of Art, Washington, D.C.
Wonderful Whimsical World of Drawing,
Herbert Palmer Gallery, Los Angeles,
California

1978
The Art of Texas, University of Chicago,
Illinois (circulated)
Four Houston Artists, Art Gallery, Florida
State University, Tallahassee
*Landscape Cityscape . . . A Survey of
Urban Landscapes in the 1970's,* Brainerd
Art Gallery, State University of New York
at Potsdam.
Painting and Sculpture Today,
Indianapolis Museum of Art, Indiana

1979
FIRE!, Contemporary Arts Museum,
Houston, Texas
Made in Texas, Archer M. Huntington
Gallery, University Art Museum,
The University of Texas at Austin
On the Right Bank of the Red River,
Root Art Center, Hamilton, New York

1980
Betty Parsons Gallery, New York City
Maryland Institute, College of Art,
Baltimore
On Paper, Institute of Contemporary Art,
Richmond, Virginia
1981
*The Image of the House in Contemporary
Art,* Lawndale Annex, University of
Houston, Texas
New York Gallery Showcase, Oklahoma
Art Center Museum, Oklahoma City
Southern Monumental Exhibition,
University Gallery, Memphis State
University, Tennessee
1982
Atomic Salon, Ronald Feldman Fine Arts
Gallery, New York City
Metropolitan Museum and Art Center,
Coral Gables, Florida
New New York, Art Gallery, Florida State
University, Talahassee
Phoenix Art Museum, Arizona
1983
Grace Borgenicht Gallery, New York City

Selected References

The Corcoran Gallery of Art, Washington,
D.C. *The 35th Biennial Exhibition of
Contemporary American Painting,*
Feb. 26-Apr. 3, 1977. Essay by Jane
Livingston.

New Orleans Museum of Art, Louisiana.
1977 Artists Biennial, May 28-July 3,
1977. Introduction by William A. Fagaly.
Essay by Jack L. Boulton.

Archer M. Huntington Gallery, University
Art Museum, The University of Texas at
Austin. *Made in Texas,* May 20-Aug. 26,
1979. Introduction by Becky Duval Reese.
Essays by Janet Kutner and Tom Livesay.

Lawndale Annex, University of Houston,
Texas. *The Image of the House in
Contemporary Art,* Nov. 8-Dec. 4, 1981.
Foreword by Charmaine Locke. Essay by
William Simon.

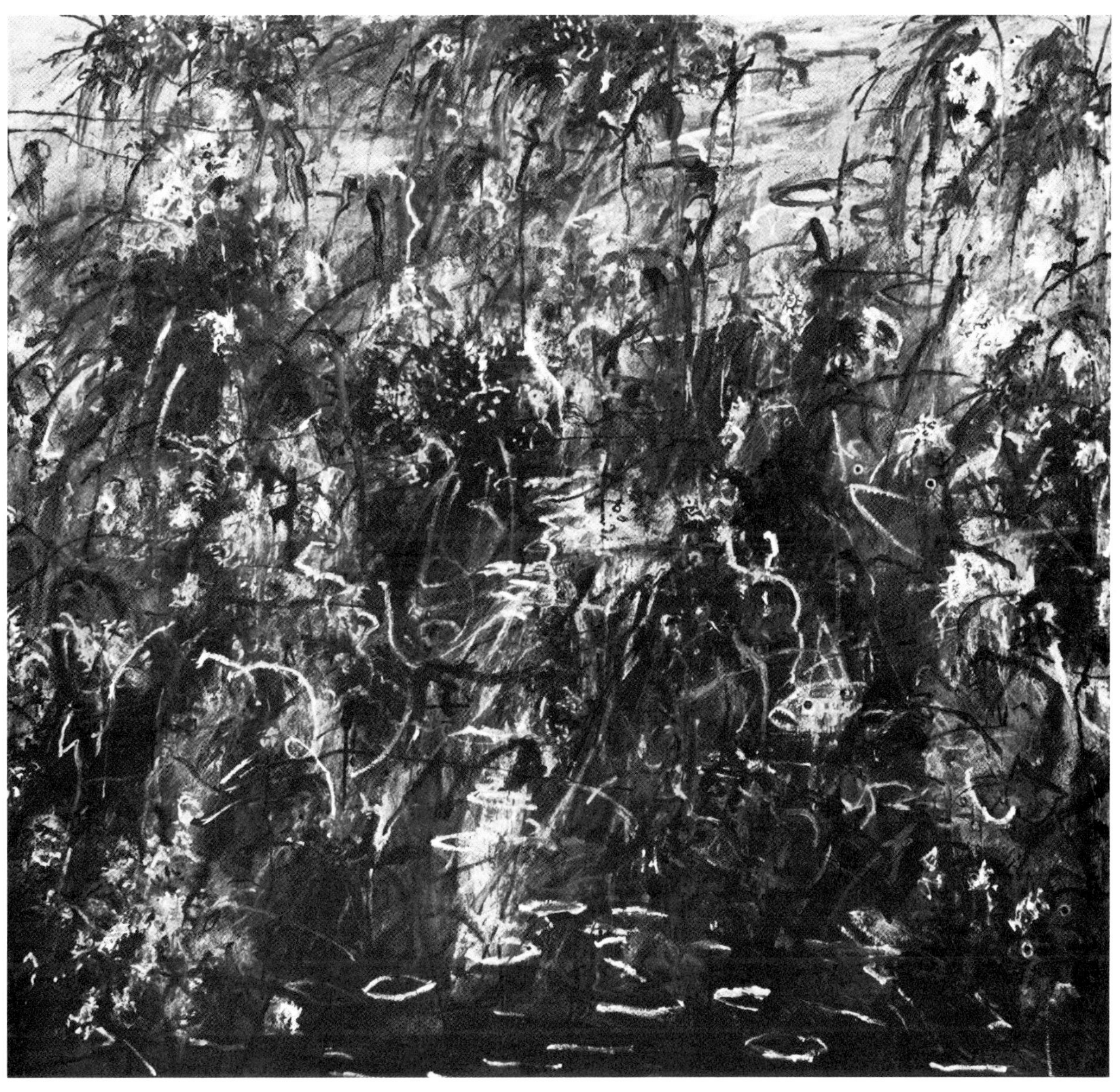

Flora, Fauna and Family Affairs 1982
Oil on canvas
78 × 84"
Collection Joanna Rogers, Dallas, Texas

David Bates

1952
Born, Dallas, Texas
1975
B.F.A., Southern Methodist University, Dallas, Texas
1977
M.F.A., Southern Methodist University, Dallas, Texas
Independent Study Program, Whitney Museum of American Art, New York City

Since 1977, Bates has been an art instructor at Eastfield College in Dallas, Texas. He lives and works in Dallas.

Awards

1982
Anne Giles Kimbrough Fund Artists' Grant, Dallas Museum of Fine Arts, Texas

Selected Solo Exhibitions

1974
David McCullough Studios, Dallas, Texas
1976
Allen Street Gallery, Dallas, Texas
1978
Eastfield College, Dallas, Texas
Meadows Gallery, Southern Methodist University, Dallas, Texas
1981-83
DW Gallery, Dallas, Texas

Selected Group Exhibitions

1974
Annual Southwest Exhibition, Fort Worth Art Museum, Texas
1975
Delahunty Gallery, Dallas, Texas
1976
Meadows Gallery, Southern Methodist University, Dallas, Texas
1977
DW Gallery, Dallas, Texas
1978
Annual Southwest Painting and Sculpture Exhibition, Laguna Gloria Art Museum, Austin, Texas
Eastfield College, Dallas, Texas
1982
Black on White, DW Gallery, Dallas, Texas
Book/Art, DW Gallery, Dallas, Texas
Fun and Games, The Art Center, Waco, Texas
1983
1983 New Orleans Triennial, New Orleans Museum of Art, Louisiana
The 38th Corcoran Biennial and 2nd Western States Exhibition, The Corcoran Gallery of Art, Washington, D.C. (circulated)
Touch with Your Eyes, Feel with Your Mind: Surfaces in Contemporary Art, Laguna Gloria Art Museum, Austin, Texas

Selected References

The Corcoran Gallery of Art, Washington, D.C. *The 38th Corcoran Biennial and 2nd Western States Exhibition,* Feb. 3-Apr. 3, 1983. Introduction by Clair List.

New Orleans Museum of Art, Louisiana. *1983 New Orleans Triennial,* Apr. 8-May 22, 1983. Introduction by William A. Fagaly. Essay by Linda L. Cathcart.

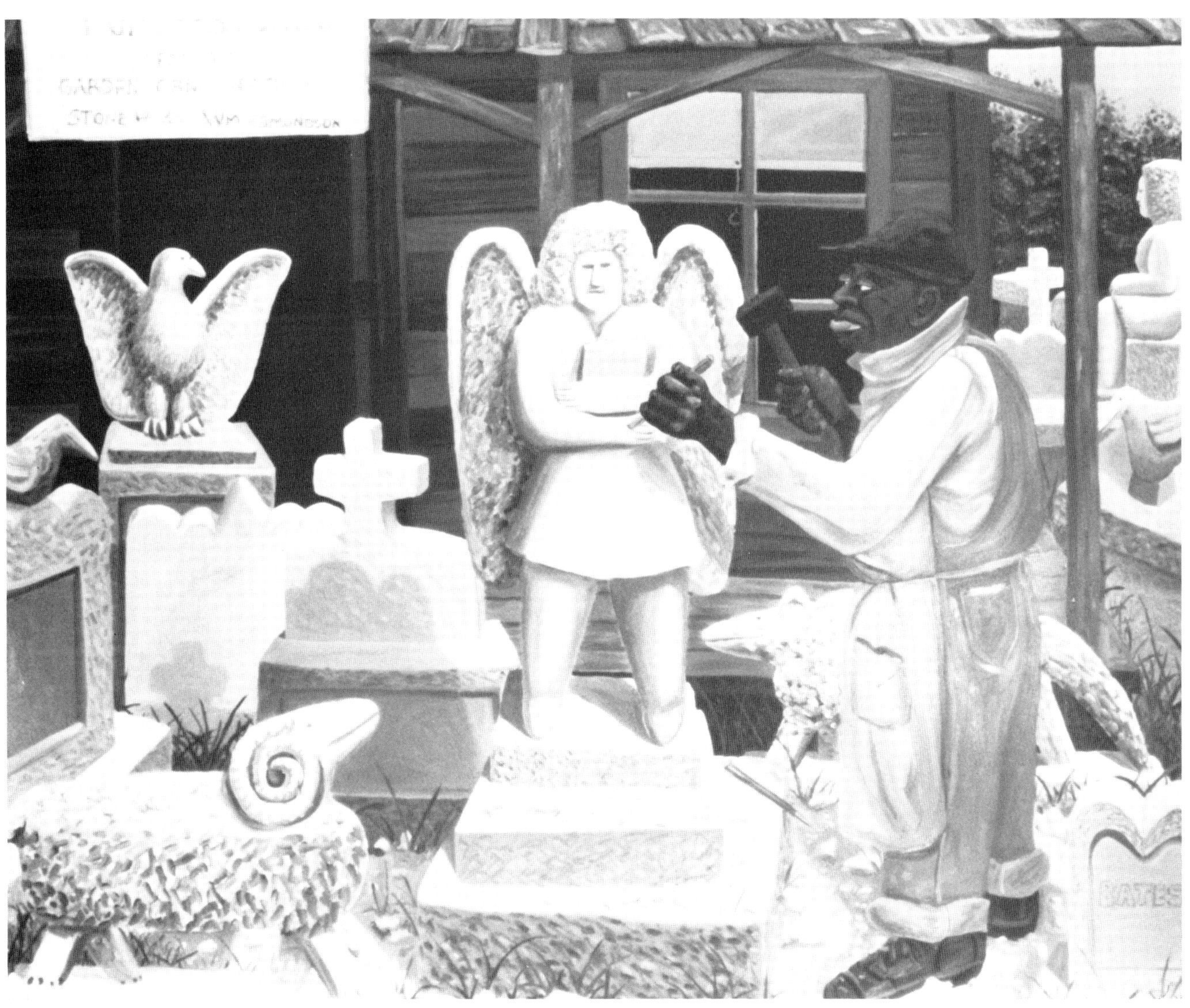

The Sculptor 1983
Oil on canvas
78 × 96″
Courtesy the artist and
Charles Cowles Gallery, New York City

Donald Beason

1943
Born, Camden, Arkansas
1965
B.A., Stephen F. Austin University, Nacogdoches, Texas
1967
M.F.A., Michigan State University, East Lansing

The artist has been an associate professor at Stephen F. Austin University in Nacogdoches, Texas, since 1967. He lives and works in Nacogdoches.

Awards

1972
Fulbright-Hays Award
1982
Individual Artists' Fellowship, National Endowment for the Arts

Selected Solo Exhibitions

1969
Gallery 107, Nacogdoches, Texas
1977
Longview Museum and Arts Center, Texas
1979
The One Seguin Arts Center, Seguin, Texas
1981
Art Museum of South Texas, Corpus Christi

Selected Group Exhibitions

1968
Jewish Community Center, Houston, Texas
1970
Drawing USA/71, Minnesota Museum of Art, St. Paul

1971
Annual Eight State Exhibition of Painting and Sculpture, Del Mar College, Corpus Christi, Texas
1972
6th Annual National Drawing and Small Sculpture Exhibition, Del Mar College, Corpus Christi, Texas
1973
United States Information Service, United States Embassy, Rome, Italy
1974
8th Annual National Drawing and Small Sculpture Exhibition, Del Mar College, Corpus Christi, Texas
1975
9th Annual National Drawing and Small Sculpture Exhibition, Del Mar College, Corpus Christi, Texas
1977
Annual Exhibition, Beaumont Art Museum, Texas
11th Annual National Drawing and Small Sculpture Exhibition, Del Mar College, Corpus Christi, Texas
Kilgore College, Texas
1978
Beason, Fenci, Wink, Gallery 107, Nacogdoches, Texas
Longview Museum and Arts Center, Texas
1979
Kilgore College Invitational, Kilgore College, Texas
1980
Air Screen, The Julius Schmidt Invitational, Cameron University, Lawton, Oklahoma
AMST 3, Art Museum of South Texas, Corpus Christi
1981
Off the Wall, Installations and Environments by Nine Texas Artists, San Antonio Museum of Art, Texas

1982
Cameron University, Lawton, Oklahoma (installation)
Lawndale Annex, University of Houston, Texas (installation)
Marian Koogler McNay Art Institute, San Antonio, Texas (installation)
Recent Works From East Texas, Tyler Museum of Art, Texas (installation)
1983
Amarillo Art Center, Texas (installation)
Invitational '83, Longview Museum and Art Center, Texas
1983 New Orleans Triennial, New Orleans Museum of Art, Louisiana
1983 Sculpture Show, Connemara Park, Dallas, Texas

Selected References

San Antonio Museum of Art, Texas. *Off the Wall, Installations and Environments by Nine Texas Artists,* Sept. 12-Nov. 1, 1981. Introduction by Sally Boothe-Meredith.

Tyler Museum of Art, Texas. *Recent Works from East Texas,* Feb. 27-Apr. 25, 1982. Introduction by James Weaver.

New Orleans Museum of Art, Louisiana. *1983 New Orleans Triennial,* Apr. 8-May 22, 1983. Introduction by William A. Fagaly. Essay by Linda L. Cathcart.

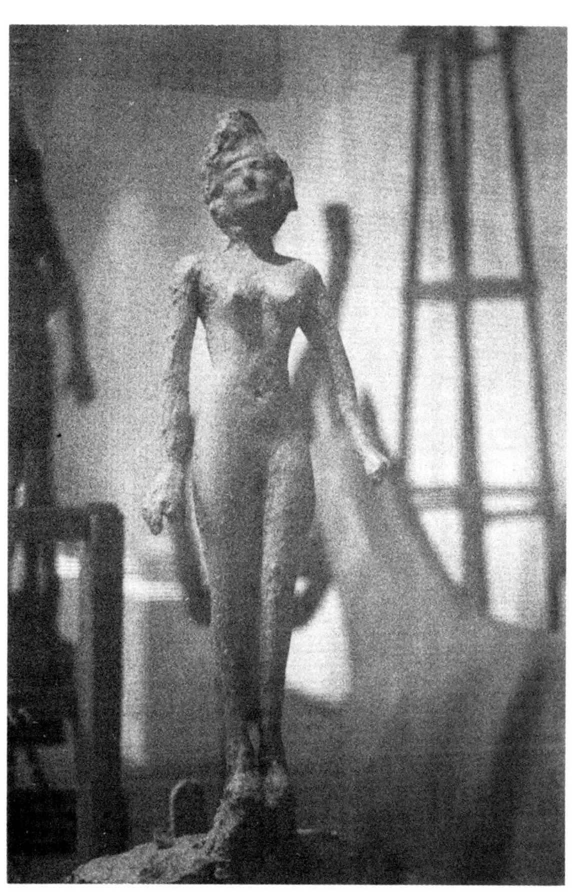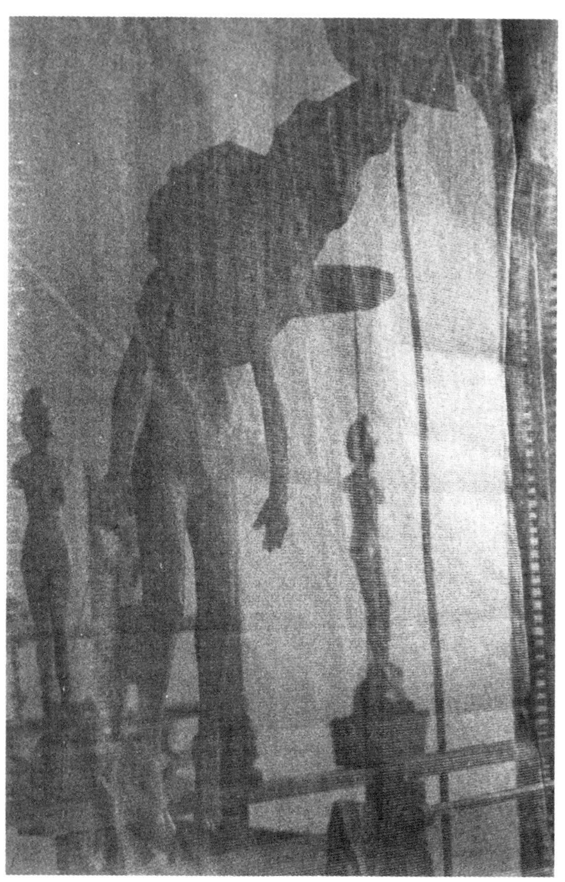

Tyler Solar Screen 1983
Installation (details)
Tyler Museum of Art, Texas

Beason's installation for the
current exhibition is *Houston-Midnight* 1983.

Derek Boshier

1937
Born, Portsmouth, England
1957
B.A., Yeovil School of Art, Royal College of Art, London, England
1962
M.F.A., Yeovil School of Art, Royal College of Art, London, England

Since 1980, the artist has been an assistant professor of Art at the University of Houston, Texas. He lives and works in Houston.

Selected Solo Exhibitions

1962
Image in Revolt, Grabowski Gallery, London, England
1965
Galerie Aujourd'hui, Brussels, Belgium
1968
Robert Fraser Gallery, London, England
1970
Nigel Greenwood Gallery, London, England
1971
Hayward Gallery, London, England
1973
Derek Boshier — Documentation and Work, 1959-1972, Whitechapel Art Gallery, London, England
1974
54 Drawings, Angela Flowers Gallery, London, England
1976
Places, Angela Flowers Gallery, London, England
1978
Events, A.I.R. Gallery, London, England
1980
Paintings and Drawings, 1979-1980, Angela Flowers Gallery, London, England
1981
Derek Boshier — Paintings, Drawings and Photographs 1961-1979, Museum of Contemporary Art, Lodz, Poland (circulated)
Derek Boshier: Paintings from 1980-1981, Contemporary Arts Museum, Houston, Texas
Drawings 1980-1981, Graham Gallery, Houston, Texas

1982
Derek Boshier — Texas Works, Institute of Contemporary Arts, London, England
Paintings and Drawings 1981-1982, Robin Cronin Inc., Houston, Texas
1983
Derek Boshier, Selected Drawings 1960-1982, Bluecoat Gallery, Liverpool, England

Selected Group Exhibitions

1959
Young Contemporaries, London, England
1961
John Moores Exhibition, Walker Art Gallery, Liverpool, England
1963
3rd Paris Biennale Des Jeunes, Museum of Modern Art, Paris, France
1964
Contemporary British Painting and Sculpture, Albright-Knox Art Gallery, Buffalo, New York
1965
Op and Pop, Samarbets Namnden for Kunstforeninger, Stockholm, Sweden
1966
Robert Fraser Gallery in Marconi, Marconi Gallery, Milan, Italy
1967
New Shapes of Colour, Stedlijk Museum, Amsterdam, the Netherlands (circulated)
1968
Six Artists, Victoria and Albert Museum, London, England
1971
Architructures, Galerie von Loeper, Hamburg, West Germany
1972
8 Artists, One Decade, Arts Council of Great Britain (circulated)
1973
Henry to Gilbert and George, Palais des Beaux Arts, Brussells, Belgium
1974
New Prints, Tate Gallery, London, England
1976
Time, Words and the Camera, Landdesmuseum Joanneum, Graz, Austria

1977
Aspects du Paysage: Oevres de dix Artistes Britanniques, British Council Exhibition, Paris, France (circulated)
1978
Art for Society, Whitechapel Art Gallery, London, England
1979
A Generation, Museum of Modern Art, Edinburgh, Scotland
1981
The Cronin Gallery, Houston, Texas
Landscape: The Printmaker's View, Tate Gallery, London, England
Six in America and Europe, Graham Gallery, Houston, Texas
1982
The Human Figure, Contemporary Arts Center, New Orleans, Louisiana
Prisoners of Conscience, Studio One, Houston, Texas
1983
Images of Texas, Archer M. Huntington Gallery, The University Art Museum, The University of Texas at Austin
1983 New Orleans Triennial, New Orleans Museum of Art, Louisiana

Selected References

Contemporary Arts Museum, Houston, Texas. *Derek Boshier: Paintings from 1980-1981*, Oct. 31-Dec. 15, 1981. Essay by Cheryl A. Brutvan.

Archer M. Huntington Gallery, University Art Museum, The University of Texas at Austin. *Images of Texas*, Feb. 25-Apr 10, 1983. Foreword by Eric S. McCready. Essay by William Goetzmann.

Bluecoat Gallery, Liverpool, England. *Derek Boshier, Selected Drawings 1960-1982*, Mar. 9-Apr. 2, 1983. Foreword by Bryan Biggs. Essay by Marco Livingston.

Institute of Contemporary Arts, London, England. *Derek Boshier — Texas Works*, Nov. 25-Jan. 9, 1983. Essay by David Brauer. Conversation by the artist.

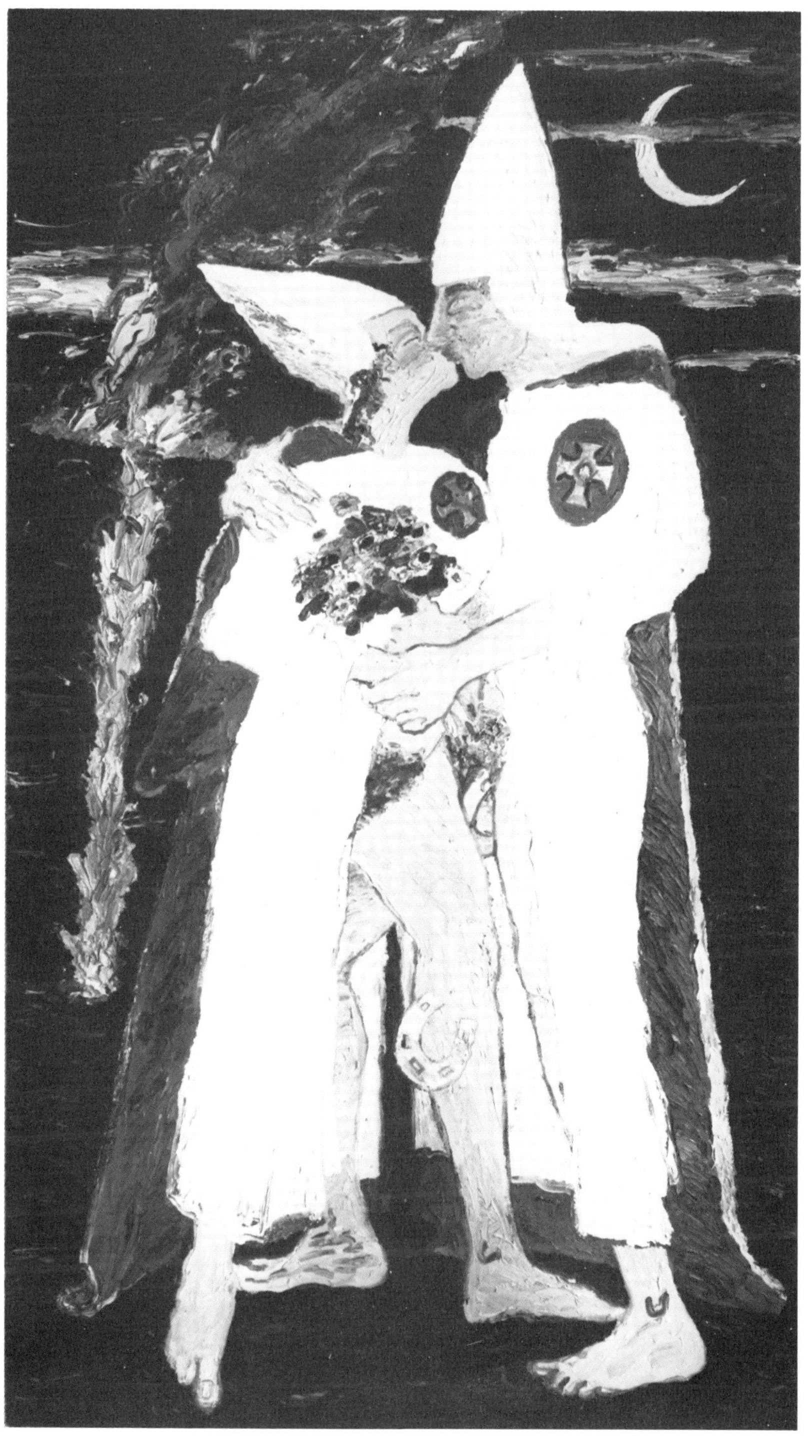

Ku Klux Klan 1982
Oil on canvas
84 × 48″
Courtesy the artist and
Texas Gallery, Houston

William Christenberry

1936
Born, Tuscaloosa, Alabama
1958
B.F.A., University of Alabama, Tuscaloosa
1959
M.A., University of Alabama, Tuscaloosa

The artist has taught at several universities, including the University of Alabama, Tuscaloosa, and Memphis State University, Tennessee. He has taught at The Corcoran School of Art, Washington, D.C., since 1968, becoming a professor there in 1974. He lives and works in Washington, D.C.

Awards

1976
Individual Artists' Fellowship, National Endowment for the Arts

Selected Solo Exhibitions

1961
University Art Gallery, University of Alabama, Tuscaloosa
1963
University Art Gallery, Memphis State University, Tennessee
1967
Mary Chil... Gallery, Memphis, Tennessee
1970
Henri Gallery, Washington, D.C.
1973
William Christenberry Photographs, The Baltimore Museum of Art, Maryland
Henri Gallery, Washington, D.C.
Jefferson Place Gallery, Washington, D.C.
1974
Henri I, Washington, D.C.
1978
William Christenberry, Color Photographs, The Corcoran Gallery of Art, Washington, D.C.
William Christenberry-Photographs, Sander Gallery, Washington, D.C.
1979
Montgomery Museum of Fine Arts, Alabama
1980
Cronin Gallery, Houston, Texas
Sander Gallery, Washington, D.C.

1981
Middendorf/Lane Gallery, Washington, D.C.
1982
Institute for the Arts, Rice University, Houston, Texas
Morgan Gallery, Kansas City, Missouri
1983
The Corcoran Gallery of Art, Washington, D.C.

Selected Group Exhibitions

1969
The Washington Painters, Ringling Museum of Art, Sarasota, Florida
1970
Drawings and Small Works, Washington Gallery of Modern Art, Washington, D.C.
Washington: Twenty Years, The Baltimore Museum of Art, Maryland
1971
Transparent and Translucent Art, Museum of Fine Arts of St. Petersburg, Florida
1972
Two Washington Sculptors, William Christenberry and Ed McGowin, J.B. Speed Museum, Louisville, Kentucky and Georgetown College, Kentucky
1973
Six Washington Photographers, Jefferson Place Gallery, Washington, D.C.
1974
Straight Color, Rochester Institute of Technology, New York
1975
Fourteen American Photographers, The Baltimore Museum of Art, Maryland (circulated)
1976
Color Photographs 1976-Christenberry, Eggleston, Gossage, Meyerowitz, Nixon, Shore, Broxton Gallery, Los Angeles, California
1977
The Contemporary American South, organized by the New Orleans Museum of Art, Louisiana, for the United States Information Agency (circulated in Europe)
10 Photographs contemporains/tendances actuelles aux Etats-Unis, Galerie Zabriskie, Paris, France

1978
Amerikanische Landschaftsphotographie, Die Neu Sammlung, Munich, West Germany
The Presence of Walker Evans, Institute of Contemporary Art, Boston, Massachusetts
1979
American Photography of the '70s, The Art Institute of Chicago, Illinois
Fotografie im Alltag Amerikas, Das Kunsigewerbemuseum, Zurich, Switzerland
1981
The New Color: A Decade of Color Photography, International Center of Photography, New York City
1982
The Image of the House in Contemporary Art, Lawndale Annex, University of Houston, Texas
Photography: The Formalist Vision, Institute of Contemporary Art, University of Pennsylvania, Philadelphia
Poetic Objects, Washington Project for the Arts, Washington, D.C.
1983
Contemporary Photographs from the Museum's Collection, Alfred C. Glassell Jr. School of Art, The Museum of Fine Arts, Houston, Texas

Selected References

The Baltimore Museum of Art, Maryland. *Fourteen American Photographers,* Jan. 21-Mar. 2, 1975. Foreword by Tom Freudenheim. Introduction by Renato Danese.

The Corcoran Gallery of Art, Washington, D.C. *William Christenberry, Color Photographs,* Dec. 21, 1978-Feb. 11, 1979. Essay by Jane Livingston.

Lawndale Annex, University of Houston, Texas. *The Image of the House in Contemporary Art,* Nov. 8-Dec. 4, 1981. Foreword by Charmaine Locke. Essay by William Simon.

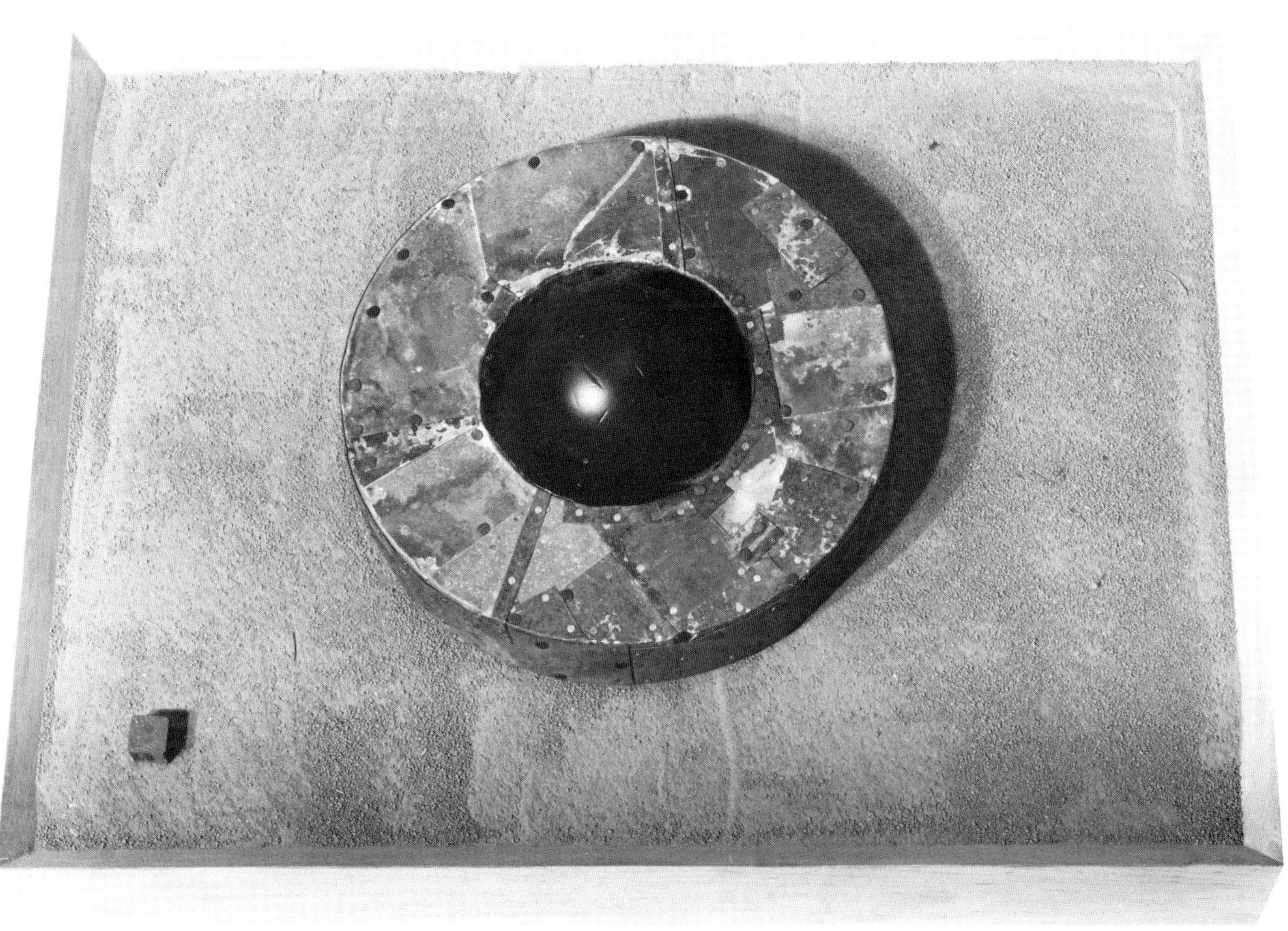

Southern Monument XII (Shiloh) 1982
Mixed media with Alabama red soil
6 × 17¹/₂ × 23″
Courtesy Moody Gallery, Houston, Texas

Rebecca Davenport

1943
Born, Alexandria, Virginia
1970
B.F.A., Pratt Institute, Brooklyn, New York
1973
M.F.A., University of North Carolina, Greensboro

The artist lives and works in Washington, D.C.

Awards

1971
Graduate Fellowship Grant,
Virginia Museum of Fine Arts, Richmond
1978
Artist Fellowship Grant,
Virginia Museum of Fine Arts, Richmond
1979
Individual Artists' Fellowship,
National Endowment for the Arts

Selected Solo Exhibitions

1973
Virginia Museum of Fine Arts, Richmond
1974
Chrysler Museum, Norfolk, Virginia
Pyramid Galleries, Ltd., Washington, D.C.
1976
Pyramid Galleries, Ltd., Washington, D.C.
1979
Fendrick Gallery, Washington, D.C.
1980
Rebecca Davenport, Aberbach Fine Art,
New York City
Osuna Gallery, Washington, D.C.
1983
Aberbach Fine Art, New York City

Selected Group Exhibitions

1970-1971
Southeastern Artists, Gallery of
Contemporary Arts, Winston-Salem,
North Carolina
1971
Virginia Artists 1971, Virginia Museum of
Fine Arts, Richmond

1972
The Figure, Pyramid Galleries, Ltd.,
Washington, D.C.
1973
11 From Washington, 55 Mercer Street,
New York City
Weatherspoon Art Gallery, Greensboro,
North Carolina
Virginia Artists 1973, Virginia Museum of
Fine Arts, Richmond
1974
Washington Figurative Artists, The
Corcoran Gallery of Art, Washington, D.C.
1976
Contemporary American Painters, Miami
Art Center, Florida
Four Young Realists, ACA Gallery, New
York City
The Liberation: 14 American Artists,
organized by The Corcoran Gallery of Art,
Washington, D.C., for the United States
Information Agency (circulated in Europe)
IX Festival International de la Peinture,
Cagnes-sur-Mer, France
300 Years of American Art, Chrysler
Museum, Norfolk, Virginia
Washington in Philadelphia, Marian Locks
Gallery, Philadelphia, Pennsylvania
1978
Selected 20th Century Nudes, Harold
Reed Gallery, New York City
X Festival International de la Peinture,
Cagnes-sur-Mer, France
Washington Realists, Middendorf/Lane
Gallery, Washington, D.C.
1979
Peaceable Kingdom, Fendrick Gallery,
Washington, D.C.
Small Works, Middendorf/Lane Gallery,
Washington, D.C.
Summer at Osuna, Osuna Gallery,
Washington, D.C.
1980
Images of the 70's: 9 Washington Artists,
The Corcoran Gallery of Art, Washington,
D.C.

1981
*Contemporary American Realism Since
1960,* Pennsylvania Academy of Fine Art,
Philadelphia (circulated)
Inside/Out: The Self Beyond Likeness,
Newport Harbor Art Museum, Newport
Beach, California (circulated)
Real, Really Real, Superreal, San Antonio
Museum of Art, Texas (circulated)
1983
Basel International Art Fair, Switzerland

Selected References

The Corcoran Gallery of Art, Washington,
D.C. *Images of the 70's: 9 Washington
Artists,* Jan. 18-Mar. 16, 1980. Preface by
Peter Marzio. Introduction and interviews
with the artists by Clair List.

Aberbach Fine Art, New York City.
Rebecca Davenport, Sept. 10-Nov. 8,
1980. Essay by Cedrick Reynolds.

San Antonio Art Association, Texas. *Real,
Really Real, Superreal,* Mar. 26-Apr. 21,
1981. Introduction by Sally Boothe-
Meredith. Essays by Alvin Martin, Linda
Nochlin and Philip Pearlstein.

Newport Harbor Art Museum, Newport
Beach, California. *Inside/Out: The Self
Beyond Likeness,* May 22-July 12, 1981.
Introduction by Cathleen S. Gallander.
Essays by Victoria Kogan and Lynn
Gamwell.

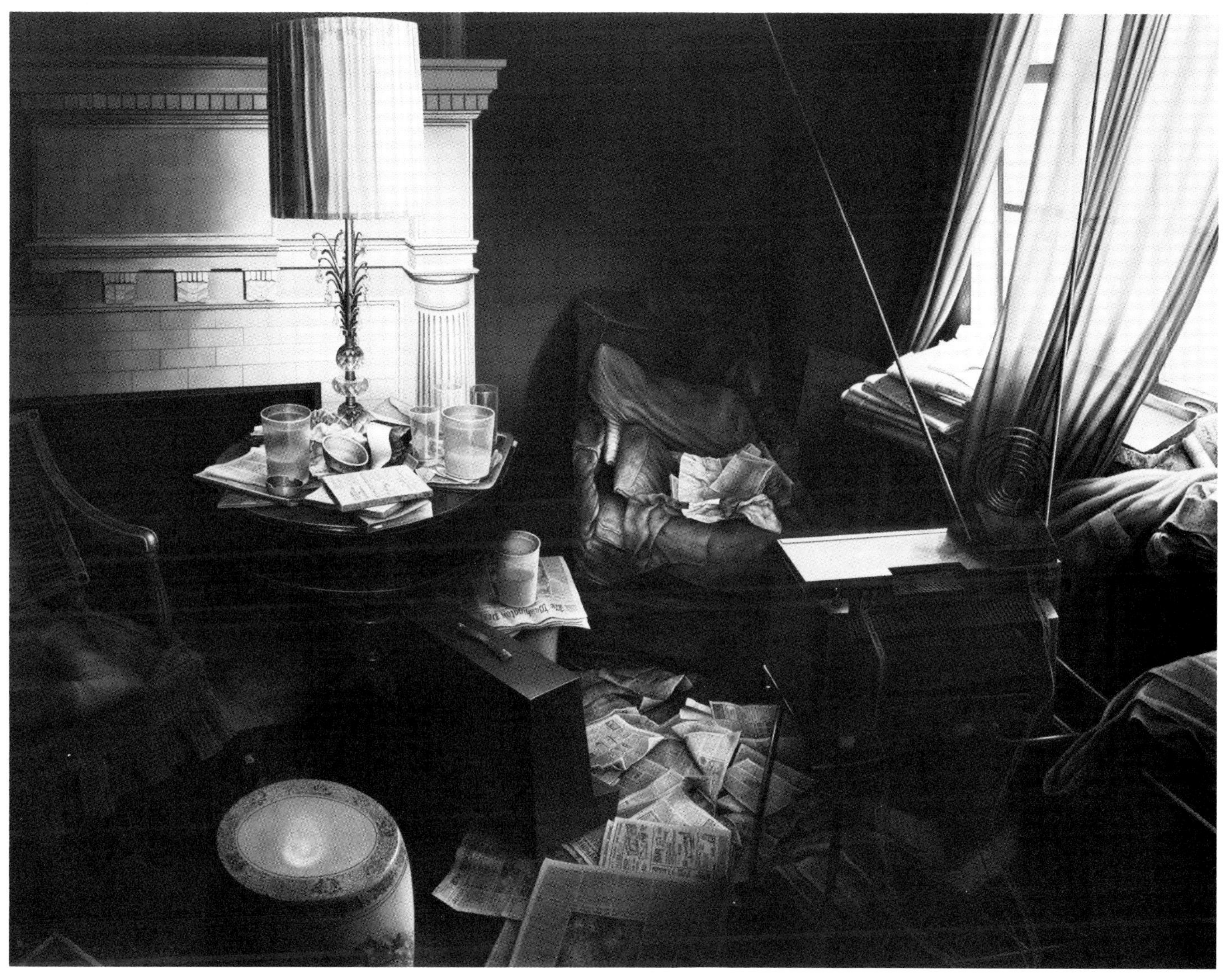

Mr. Harris 1979
Oil on canvas
72 × 96″
Collection Hanoj and Myrna Perez,
North Miami Beach, Florida

James Drake

1946
Born, Lubbock, Texas
1969
B.F.A., Art Center College of Design,
Los Angeles, California
1970
M.F.A., Art Center College of Design,
Los Angeles, California

The artist lives and works in El Paso,
Texas.

Selected Solo Exhibitions

1971
The University of Texas at El Paso
1976
Museo de Arte Y Historia, Ciudad Juarez,
Mexico
The Pavilion Art Gallery, Scottsdale,
Arizona
1981
Abilene Fine Arts Museum, Texas
El Paso Museum of Art, Texas
*New Visions: 1981, James Drake:
Sculptor,* Amarillo Art Center, Texas
Wichita Falls Museum and Art Center,
Texas
1982
Galveston Arts Center on the Strand,
Texas
Robert Speaker Gallery, Los Angeles,
California
The University of Texas at El Paso

Selected Group Exhibitions

1967
12th Annual Sun Carnival Exhibition,
El Paso Museum of Art, Texas
1968
Butler Institute of Art, Youngstown, Ohio
1970
Cerritos College Annual Exhibition,
California
1971
Long Beach Museum of Art, California
1974
Jersey City Art Museum, New Jersey
33rd Annual Exhibit, The Painters and
Sculptors Society of New Jersey, New
York City
1975
International Biennial of Graphic of Art,
Museum of Modern Art, Ljubljana,
Yugoslavia
1976
Art Exhibition Peace, 75 3 Ouno, Slovenj
Gradec, Yugoslavia
21st Annual Sun Carnival Exhibition,
El Paso Museum of Art, Texas
*Primo Internazionale Biella Per L,
Incisione,* Biella, Italy
1977
*7th National Print and Drawing
Exhibition,* Minot State College,
North Dakota
1978
Visual Arts Center of Alaska, Anchorage
1979
International Designer Craftsman,
El Paso Museum of Art, Texas
Made in Texas, Archer M. Huntington
Gallery, University Art Museum,
The University of Texas at Austin

1980
Copper II, University of Arizona
Museum of Art, Tucson
University Art Gallery, San Diego
State University, California
1981
500 Exposition Gallery, Dallas, Texas
Lawndale Annex, University of Houston,
Texas
1982
Fabric/Fiber, Texas Christian University,
Fort Worth
Fun and Games, The Art Center, Waco,
Texas
Invitational 1982, Longview Museum and
Art Center, Texas
1983
1983 New Orleans Triennial, New
Orleans Museum of Art, Louisiana

Selected References

Archer M. Huntington Gallery, University
Art Museum, The University of Texas at
Austin. *Made in Texas,* May 20-Aug. 26,
1979. Introduction by Becky Duval Reese.
Essays by Janet Kutner and Tom Livesay.

Amarillo Art Center, Texas. *New Visions:
1981, James Drake: Sculptor,* May 13-
June 21, 1981. Essay by David Turner.

New Orleans Museum of Art, Louisiana.
1983 New Orleans Triennial, Apr. 8-
May 22, 1983. Introduction by William A.
Fagaly. Essay by Linda L. Cathcart.

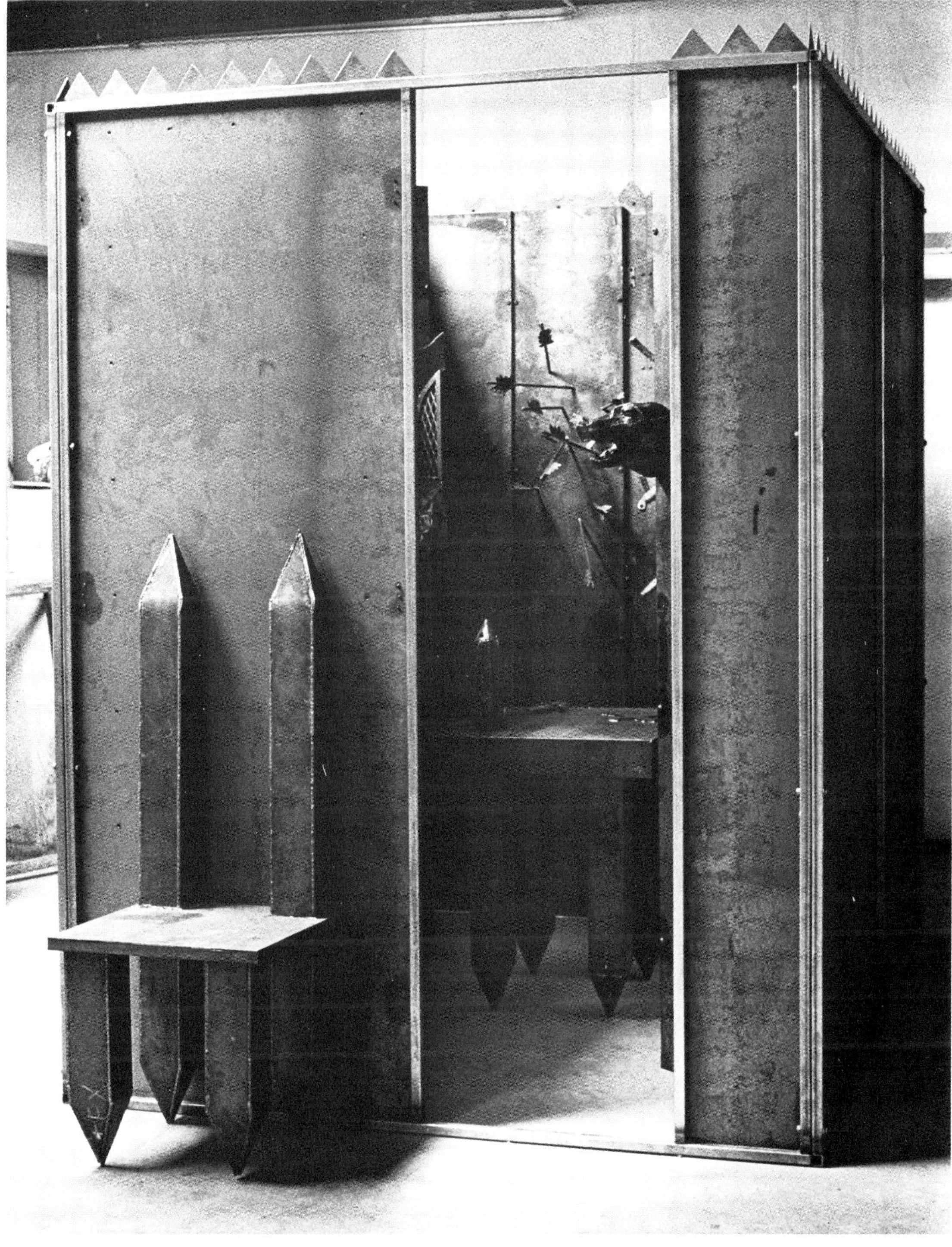

The Walk-in File Cabinet 1983
Welded steel and conti crayon
96 × 72 × 120″
Courtesy the artist

William Eggleston

1939
Born, Memphis, Tennessee

The artist lives and works in Memphis, Tennessee.

Awards

1974
John Simon Guggenheim Memorial Foundation Fellowship
1975
Individual Artists' Fellowship, National Endowment for the Arts
1980
Survey Grant Program, National Endowment for the Arts

Selected Solo Exhibitions

1974
Jefferson Place Gallery, Washington, D.C.
1976
Grapestake Gallery, San Francisco, California
Photographs by William Eggleston, The Museum of Modern Art, New York City
1977
Brooks Memorial Art Gallery, Memphis, Tennessee
Castelli Graphics/Leo Castelli Gallery, New York City
Election Eve, William Eggleston, The Corcoran Gallery of Art, Washington, D.C. (circulated)
Allan Frumkin Gallery, Chicago, Illinois
Lunn Gallery, Washington, D.C.
1979
Photographers' Gallery, Melbourne, Australia
Volkhochschule, Berlin, West Germany
1980
Charles Cowles Gallery, New York City
1982
Lunn Gallery, Washington, D.C.
1983
Werkstatt fur Photographie, Berlin, West Germany

Selected Group Exhibitions

1974
Art Now '74, John F. Kennedy Center for the Performing Arts, Washington, D.C.
1975
Fourteen American Photographers, The Baltimore Museum of Art, Maryland (circulated)
1977
The Contemporary South, organized by the New Orleans Museum of Art, Louisiana for the United States Information Agency (circulated in Europe)
Contemporary American Photographic Works, The Museum of Fine Arts, Houston, Texas
Some Color Photographs, Castelli Graphics, New York City
1978
Amerikanische Landschafstphotographie, Die Neu Sammlung, Munich, West Germany
Mirrors and Windows, The Museum of Modern Art, New York City
Photographs from the Collection of Sam Wagstaff, The Corcoran Gallery of Art, Washington, D.C.
23 Photographiers, 23 Directions, Walker Art Gallery, Liverpool, England
1979
American Photography in the 1970's, The Art Institute of Chicago, Illinois
One of a Kind, The Museum of Fine Arts, Houston, Texas
1980
Nuages, Bibliotheque Nationale, Paris France
1981
Color in Contemporary Photography, University Museum, Southern Illinois University, Carbondale
1982
Target III: In Sequence, The Museum of Fine Arts, Houston, Texas

Selected References

The Baltimore Museum of Art, Maryland. *Fourteen American Photographers,* Jan. 21-Mar. 2, 1975. Foreword by Tom Freudenheim. Introduction by Renato Danese.

The Museum of Modern Art, New York City. *William Eggleston's Guide,* May 24-Aug. 1, 1976. Essay by John Szarkowski.

The Corcoran Gallery of Art, Washington, D.C. *Election Eve, William Eggleston,* Dec. 10, 1977-Jan. 22, 1978. Essay by Jane Livingston.

The Museum of Fine Arts, Houston, Texas. *Target III: In Sequence,* July 23-Sept. 19, 1982. Introduction by Anne Wilkes Tucker. Essay by Leroy Searle.

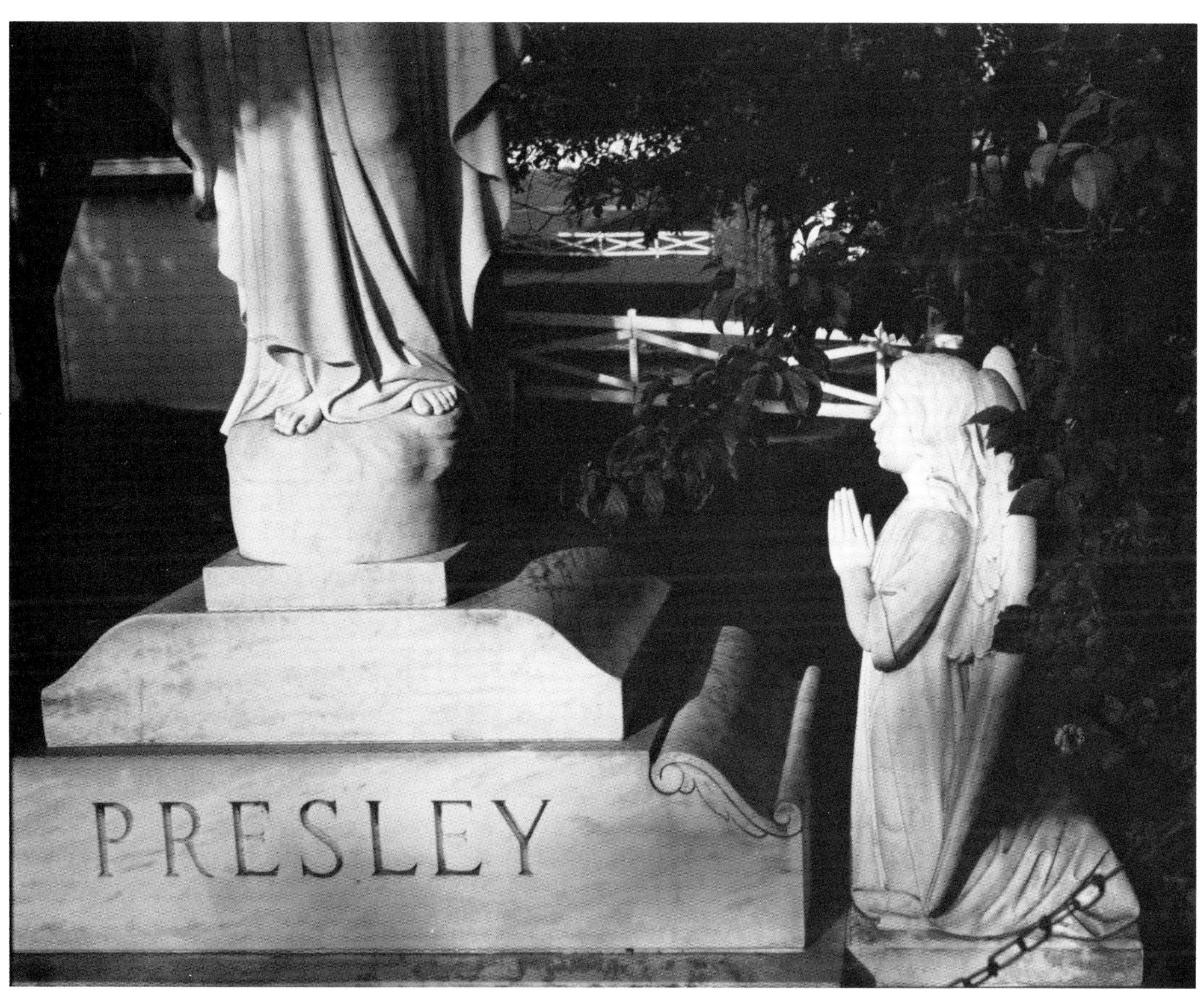

Graceland 1983
Dye-transfer print
20 × 24"
Courtesy the artist and
Middendorf Gallery, Washington, D.C.

Vernon Fisher

1943
Born, Fort Worth, Texas
1967
B.A., Hardin-Simmons University, Abeline, Texas
1969
M.F.A., University of Illinois, Champaign-Urbana

The artist has taught at several universities, including Austin College, Sherman, Texas. He taught at North Texas State University, Denton, from 1978 to 1981. He lives and works in Fort Worth, Texas.

Awards

1974, 1980, 1981
Individual Artists' Fellowship, National Endowment for the Arts

Selected Solo Exhibitions

1970
North Texas State University, Denton
1973
123456 Vernon Fisher, Tyler Museum of Art, Texas
1975
Delahunty Gallery, Dallas, Texas
1976
Drawings 1974-76, The University of Texas at Arlington
William Sawyer Gallery, San Francisco, California
1977
Paintings, Drawings and Photographs, Delahunty Gallery, Dallas, Texas
1979
Delahunty Gallery, Dallas, Texas
1980
Barbara Gladstone Gallery, New York City
Breaking the Code, Franklin Furnace, New York City
Vernon Fisher: Story Paintings and Drawings, Contemporary Arts Museum, Houston, Texas
1982
Delahunty Gallery, Dallas, Texas
Galerie T'Venster, Rotterdam, the Netherlands

Selected Group Exhibitions

1968
13th Annual Sun Carnival Exhibition, El Paso Museum of Art, Texas
1969
Rosner Gallery, Chicago, Illinois
1970
Project South/Southwest: Younger American Artists, Fort Worth Art Museum, Texas
1971
Tarrant County 34th Exhibition, Fort Worth Art Museum, Texas
1972
Exhibition of Ten Texas Painters, Art Museum of South Texas, Corpus Christi
1973
Texas Drawing Exhibition, Smither Gallery, Dallas, Texas
1974
Delahunty Gallery, Dallas, Texas
Henri Gallery, Washington, D.C.
1975
Exchange DFW/SFO, Fort Worth Art Museum, Texas (circulated)
1976
Invitational Miniature Exhibition, DW Gallery, Dallas, Texas
1977
American Narrative/Story Art 1967-77, Contemporary Arts Museum, Houston, Texas (circulated)
Six Painters Southwest, Museum of Art, University of Oklahoma, Norman
1978
Chandelier, Delahunty Gallery, Dallas, Texas
Corsicana Panorama, Corsicana Warehouse Living Arts Center, Texas
Cowboys, Indians and Settlers, Waco Art Center, Texas
1979
FIRE!, Contemporary Arts Museum, Houston, Texas
Made in Texas, Archer M. Huntington Gallery, University Art Museum, The University of Texas at Austin

1980
Basel ART 11, The International Art Fair, Basel, Switzerland
Investigations: Probe/Structure/Analysis, The New Museum, New York City
Response, Tyler Museum of Art, Texas
1981
Directions 1981, Hirshhorn Museum and Sculpture Garden, Smithsonian Institution, Washington, D.C.
19 Artists-Emergent Americans: 1981 Exxon National Exhibition, The Solomon R. Guggenheim Museum, New York City
1981 Biennial Exhibition, Whitney Museum of American Art, New York City
The Southern Voice: Terry Allen, Vernon Fisher, Ed McGowin, Fort Worth Art Museum, Texas
A Texas Group Show, Charles Cowles Gallery, New York City
1982
Fifth India Triennial, New Delhi
Still Modern After All These Years, Chrysler Museum, Norfolk, Virginia
Texas on Paper, Contemporary Arts Museum, Houston, Texas (circulated)
1983
The 38th Corcoran Biennial and 2nd Western States Exhibition, The Corcoran Gallery of Art, Washington, D.C.

Selected References

Contemporary Arts Museum, Houston, Texas. *Vernon Fisher: Story Paintings and Drawings.* Nov. 22, 1980-Jan. 4, 1981. Essay by Marti Mayo.

Tyler Museum of Art, Texas. *Response,* Feb. 9-Mar. 23, 1980. Introduction by Ron Gleason.

The New Museum, New York City. *Investigations: Probe/Structure/Analysis,* Sept. 27-Dec. 4, 1980. Essays by Lynn Gumpert and Allan Swartzman.

The Corcoran Gallery of Art, Washington, D.C. *The 38th Corcoran Biennial Exhibition and 2nd Western States Exhibition,* Feb. 3-Apr. 3, 1983. Introduction by Clair List.

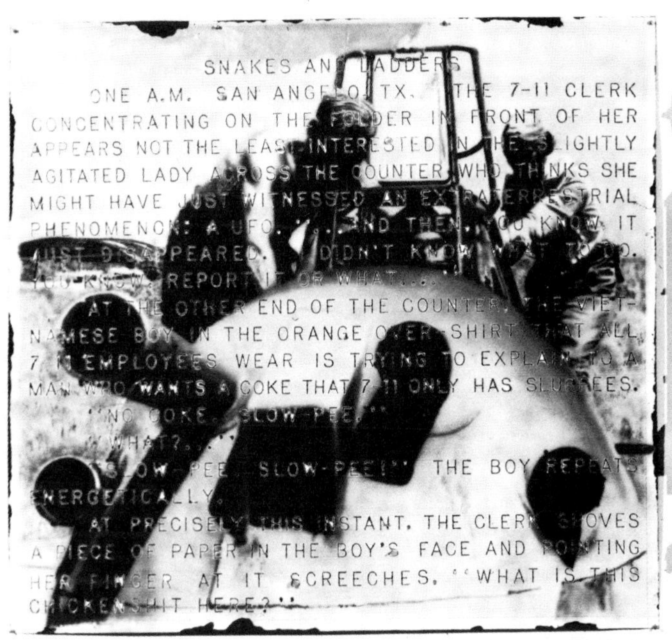

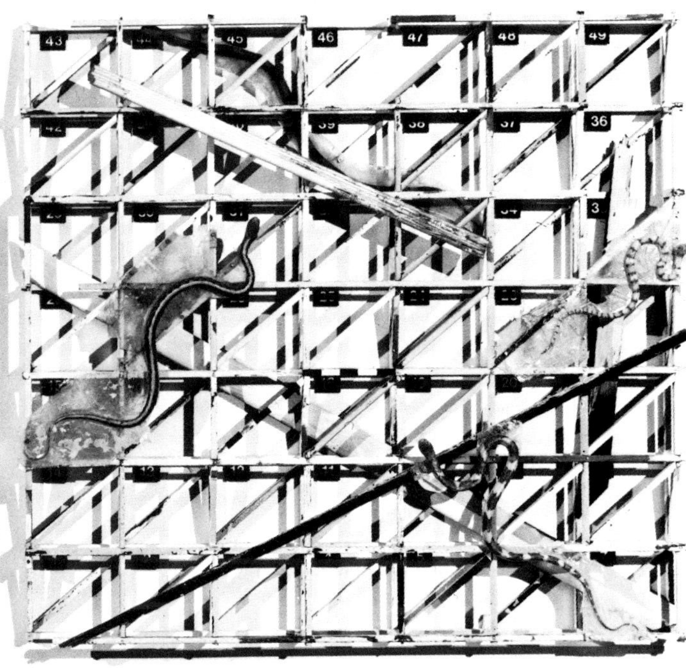

Snakes and Ladders 1982
Mixed media
135 × 59 × 6″
Collection Robert K. Hoffman,
Dallas, Texas

Roy Fridge

1927
Born, Beeville, Texas
1950
B.A., Baylor University, Waco, Texas

In 1969, the artist organized the Filmmaking Department at the Art School of the University of Oklahoma, Norman and taught there until 1973. He presently lives and works in Victoria, Texas.

Selected Solo Exhibitions

1957
Baylor Theater, Waco, Texas
1959
The Art Center, Waco, Texas
1966-1968
David Gallery, Houston, Texas
1976
Robinson Galleries, Houston, Texas
1977
DW Gallery, Dallas, Texas
1978
Reflections of an Amateur Hermit, Art Museum of South Texas, Corpus Christi
1980
Souvenirs of the Voyage, Moody Gallery, Houston, Texas
1982
Conversations from the Woods, Moody Gallery, Houston, Texas

Selected Group Exhibitions

1958
Humor in Art, Dallas Museum for Contemporary Art, Texas
1960
Haydon Calhoun Gallery, Dallas, Texas
1961
The Art That Broke the Looking Glass, Dallas Museum for Contemporary Art, Texas
1962
Haydon Calhoun Gallery, Dallas, Texas
1965
David Gallery, Houston, Texas
1966
Grand Ballroom, Rice Memorial Center, Rice University, Houston, Texas
Made of Iron, University of St. Thomas, Houston, Texas

1967
Six Sculptors, Jewish Community Center, Houston, Texas
1968
Atelier Chapman Kelly, Dallas, Texas
1971
One i at a Time, Meadows Gallery, Southern Methodist University, Dallas, Texas
1975
Artists Make Toys, Art Museum of South Texas, Corpus Christi
1976
Altered Image, Texas Agricultural & Mechanical University, Corpus Christi
Sewall Art Gallery, Rice University, Houston, Texas
1977
Installations for Corner Spaces, Fort Worth Art Museum, Texas
1979
FIRE!, Contemporary Arts Museum, Houston, Texas
Wood in Art, The Museum of Fine Arts, Houston, Texas
1980
Response, Tyler Museum of Art, Texas
1981
The Image of the House in Contemporary Art, Lawndale Annex, University of Houston, Texas
Inside/Out: The Self Beyond Likeness, Newport Harbor Art Museum, Newport Beach, California (circulated)
1982
The Americans: The Collage, Contemporary Arts Museum, Houston, Texas
Art from Houston in Norway, Stavanger Kunstforening, Norway
Poetic Objects, Washington Project for the Arts, Washington, D.C.
Shrines/Altars, Objects Gallery, San Antonio, Texas

1983
A Partial Look: Selected Works from the Corporate Collection of Atlantic Richfield Company, Dallas, Texas, Art Museum of South Texas, Corpus Christi
Contemporary Images: Thirteen South Texas Artists, Cayman Gallery, New York City
Fact and Fiction: New Work by James Surls, Roy Fridge, Ed Blackburn, Vernon Fisher, Aspen Center for the Visual Arts, Colorado

Selected References

Stavanger Kunstforening, Norway. *Art from Houston in Norway,* June 3-28, 1982. Introduction by David Brauer.

Contemporary Arts Museum, Houston, Texas. *The Americans: The Collage,* July 11-Oct. 3, 1982. Foreword and essay by Linda L. Cathcart.

Aspen Center for the Visual Arts, Colorado. *Fact and Fiction: New Work by James Surls, Roy Fridge, Ed Blackburn, Vernon Fisher,* Mar. 12-Apr. 1983. Introduction by Ron Gleason. Introduction by Susan Freudenheim.

Cayman Gallery, New York City. *Contemporary Images: Thirteen South Texas Artists,* May 5-28, 1983. Essay by William Otton.

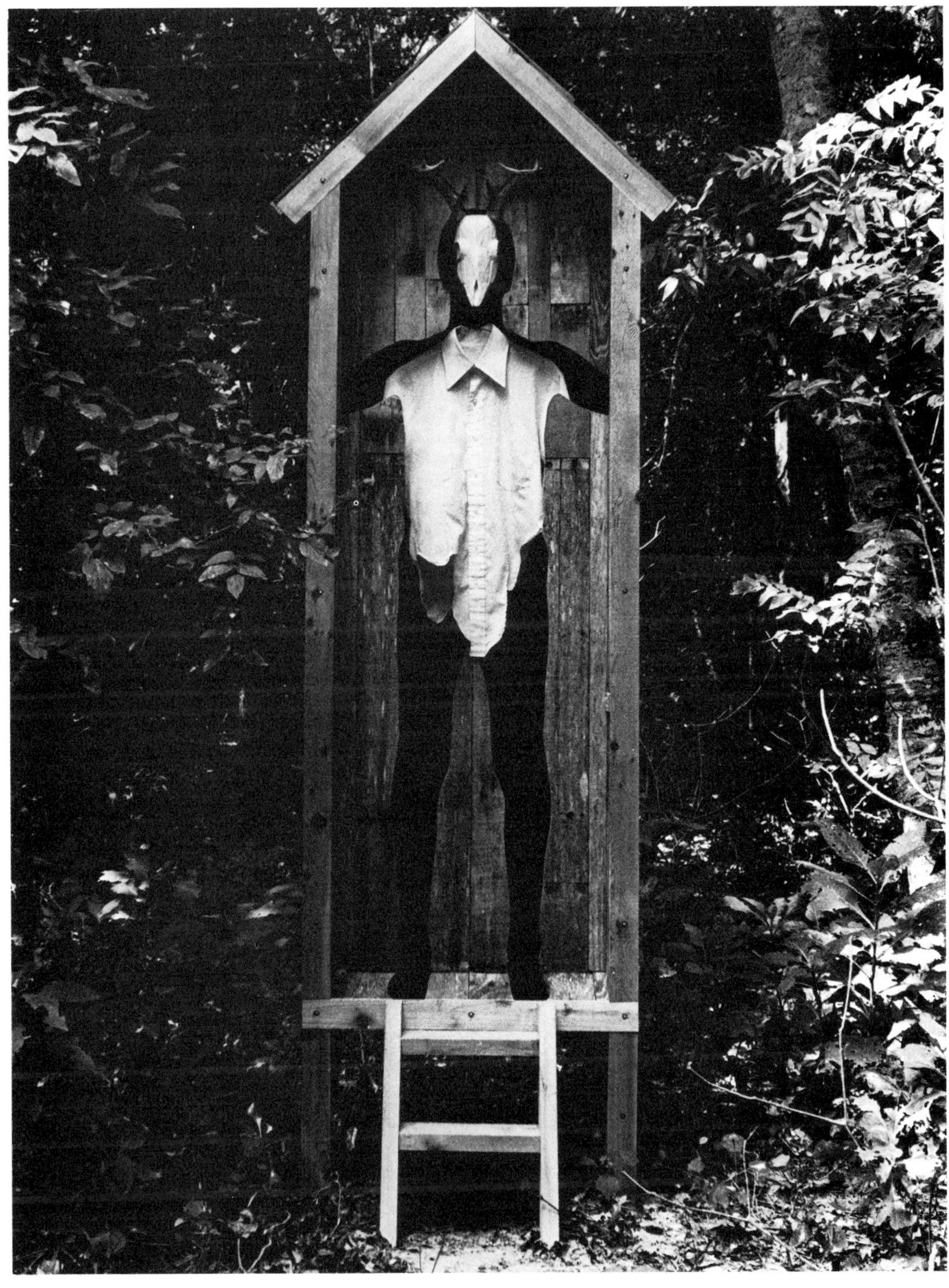

Standing Shaman Shrine 1982
Wood, cloth and deer skull mask
108 × 30 × 14″
Courtesy the artist and Moody Gallery,
Houston, Texas

Robert Gordy

1933
Born, Jefferson Island, Louisiana
1955
B.A., Louisiana State University, Baton Rouge
1956
M.A., Louisiana State University, Baton Rouge

The artist has taught at several institutions, including the University of Southwest Louisiana at Lafayette, and Louisiana State University, Baton Rouge. He lives and works in New Orleans.

Awards

1978
Individual Artists' Fellowship, National Endowment for the Arts

Selected Solo Exhibitions

1965
A. L. Lowe Gallery, New Orleans, Louisiana
1967-1968
Glade Gallery, New Orleans, Louisiana
1969-1971
Galerie Simonne Stern, New Orleans, Louisiana
1969
Recent Paintings and Drawings: Robert Gordy, Tampa Bay Art Center, Florida
1972
Isaac Delgado Museum of Art, New Orleans, Louisiana
1973
Hauk Baum Gallery, San Francisco, California
Galerie Simonne Stern, New Orleans, Louisiana
1975
Long Beach Museum of Art, California
1976
Phyllis Kind Gallery, Chicago, Illinois
1977
Delahunty Gallery, Dallas, Texas
1979
Phyllis Kind Gallery, New York City
1981
Robert Gordy, Paintings and Drawings: 1960-1980, New Orleans Museum of Art, Louisiana (circulated)

1983
Galerie Simonne Stern, New Orleans, Louisiana

Selected Group Exhibitions

1954
53rd Annual Exhibition of Art Association of New Orleans, Isaac Delgado Museum of Art, Louisiana
1957
57th Annual Exhibition of Art Association of New Orleans, Isaac Delgado Museum of Art, Louisiana
1958
58th Annual Exhibition of Art Association of New Orleans, Isaac Delgado Museum of Art, Louisiana
1959
Biennial of American Painting and Sculpture, The Detroit Institute of Arts, Michigan
1967
Annual Exhibition of American Painting and Sculpture, Whitney Museum of American Art, New York City
1968
Louisiana Gallery, Houston, Texas
New Acquisitions Show, Whitney Museum of American Art, New York City
1969
Project South-Southwest, Fort Worth Art Center, Texas
The Spirit of the Comics, Institute of Contemporary Art, University of Pennsylvania, Philadelphia
1973
Artists Biennial, New Orleans Museum of Art, Louisiana
Biennial Exhibition of Contemporary Art, Whitney Museum of American Art, New York City
Divergent Representation: Five Contemporary Artists, National Collection of Fine Arts, Washington, D.C.
1975
Art: USA: The South, organized by the New Orleans Museum of Art, Louisiana, for the U.S. Information Agency (circulated in Central and South America)
Extraordinary Realities, Whitney Museum of American Art, New York City

1976
North-East-West-South and Middle, Moore College of Art, Philadelphia, Pennsylvania (circulated)
1977
Invitational American Drawing Exhibition, Fine Arts Gallery, San Diego, California
1978
21st National Print Exhibition, The Brooklyn Museum, New York
1979
The 1970's: New American Painting, organized by The New Museum, New York City for the U.S. International Communications Agency (circulated in Eastern Europe)
1980
American Drawings in Black and White: 1970-1980, The Brooklyn Museum, New York
American Figure Painting: 1950-1980, Chrysler Museum, Norfolk, Virginia
The Figurative Tradition: Paintings and Sculpture from the Permanent Collection, Whitney Museum of American Art, New York City
Image into Pattern, Institute for Art and Urban Resources, P.S. 1, Long Island City, New York

Selected Publications

Tampa Bay Art Center, Florida. *Recent Paintings and Drawings: Robert Gordy,* May 17-June 30, 1969. Essay by Jan Aldmann.

The Brooklyn Museum, New York. *21st National Print Exhibition,* Dec. 9, 1978- Feb. 11, 1979. Introduction by Gene Baro.

The New Museum, New York City. *The 1970's: New American Painting,* June 15, 1979-Feb. 15, 1981. Essays by Allan Schwartzman, Kathleen Thomas and Marcia Tucker.

New Orleans Museum of Art, Louisiana. *Robert Gordy, Paintings and Drawings: 1960-1980.* Apr. 25-June 14, 1981. Essay by Gene Baro.

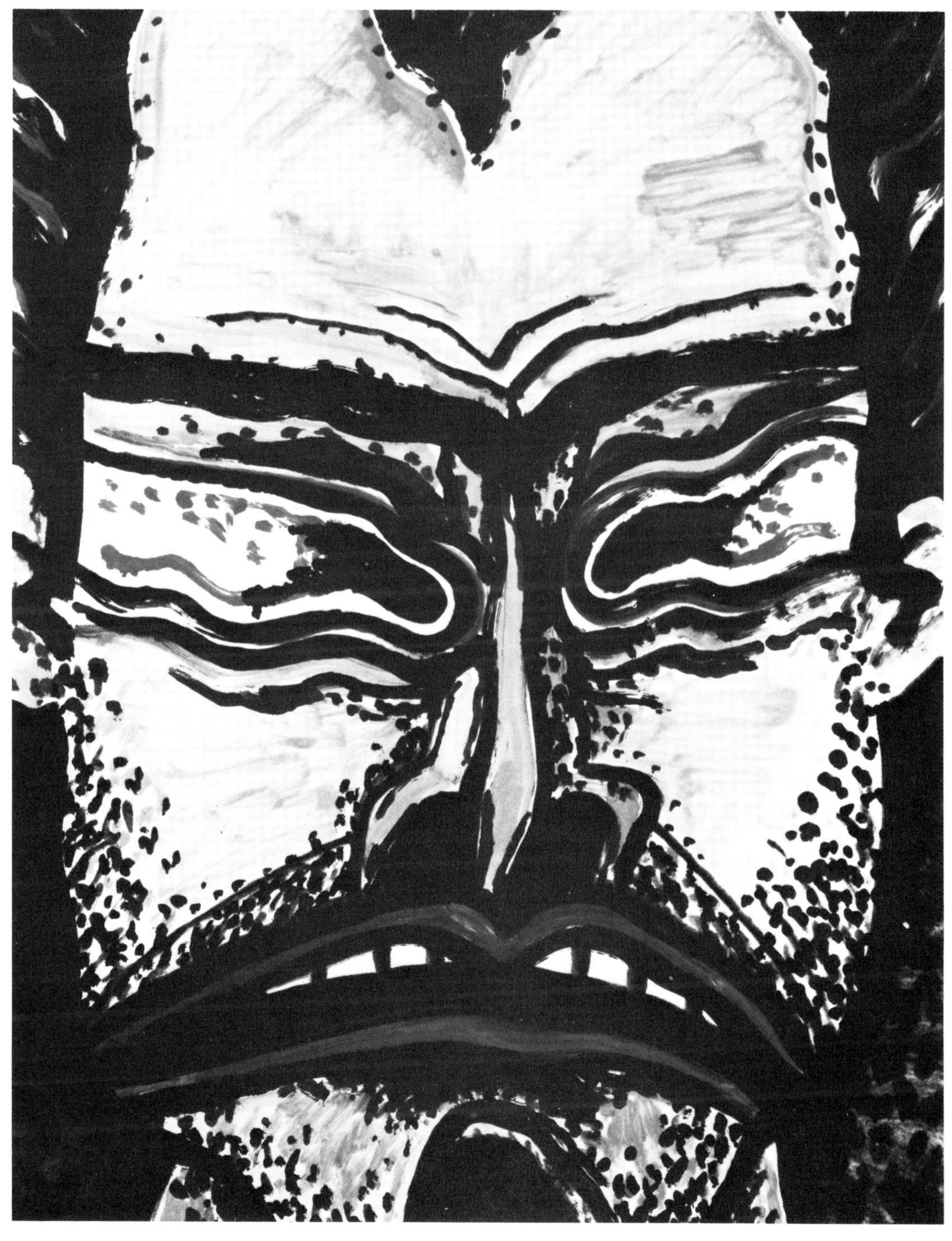

Study for "Quint" (1st version) 1982
Monoprint
19³/₄ × 15¹/₂"
Courtesy the artist

Jimmy Jalapeeno

1947
Born, Bryan, Texas
1969
B.F.A., The University of Texas at Austin
1973
M.F.A., University of California, Davis

The artist has taught at several universities including the University of Houston, Texas. He presently works as a photographer for the Texas Historical Commission, Austin, Texas. The artist lives and works in Austin.

Awards

1980
Individual Artists' Fellowship, National Endowment for the Arts

Selected Solo Exhibitions

1971
Texas Union Gallery, Austin, Texas
1972
Sacramento City College Gallery, California
1978
Young Texas Artist Series, Amarillo Art Center, Texas
1979
Austin College, Sherman, Texas
1980
Bois d'Arc Gallery, Austin, Texas
1981
Anyone Can Paint, 80 Langton Street, San Francisco, California

Selected Group Exhibitions

1972
Annual National Drawing and Sculpture Exhibition, Del Mar College, Corpus Christi, Texas
An Evening with Bean and Friends, Davis Art and Drama Departments, University of California (performance)
Manuel Neri and Friends, Western Washington State College, Bellingham
1973
Delahunty Gallery, Dallas, Texas
Invitational 1973, Longview Museum and Art Center, Texas
1976
80 Langton Street, San Francisco, California
Ine Apers Gallery, Austin, Texas
1977
O Sidewalk Thou Art in Austin, Laguna Gloria Art Museum, Austin, Texas (performance)
1978
Home Already, 80 Langton Street, San Francisco, California (performance)
1979
Made in Texas, Archer M. Huntington Gallery, University Art Museum, The University of Texas at Austin
Miniatures, Lawndale Annex, University of Houston, Texas
1980
Invitational '80, 500 Exposition Gallery, Dallas, Texas
Texas Only, Laguna Gloria Art Museum, Austin, Texas
T.V. Robinson Gallery, Houston, Texas
1981
World's Most Boring Slide Show, San Francisco State University, California (performance)
1982
Here and Now, Dougherty Cultural Arts Center, Austin, Texas
New Works, Summer 1982, Laguna Gloria Art Museum, Austin, Texas
1983
An Evening of Conceptual Art, David Amdur Gallery, Austin, Texas (performance)
1983 New Orleans Triennial, New Orleans Museum of Art, Louisiana

Selected References

Amarillo Art Center, Texas. *Young Texas Artist Series: Jimmy Jalapeeno: an Exhibition of Paintings and Drawings,* Mar. 29-Apr. 16, 1978.

Archer M. Huntington Gallery, University Art Museum, The University of Texas at Austin. *Made in Texas,* May 20-Aug. 26, 1979. Introduction by Becky Duval Reese. Essays by Janet Kutner and Tom Livesay.

Laguna Gloria Art Museum, Austin, Texas. *New Works, Summer 1982,* July 2-25, 1982. Introduction by Annette DiMeo Carlozzi.

New Orleans Museum of Art, Louisiana. *1983 New Orleans Triennial,* Apr. 8-May 22, 1983. Introduction by William A. Fagaly. Essay by Linda L. Cathcart.

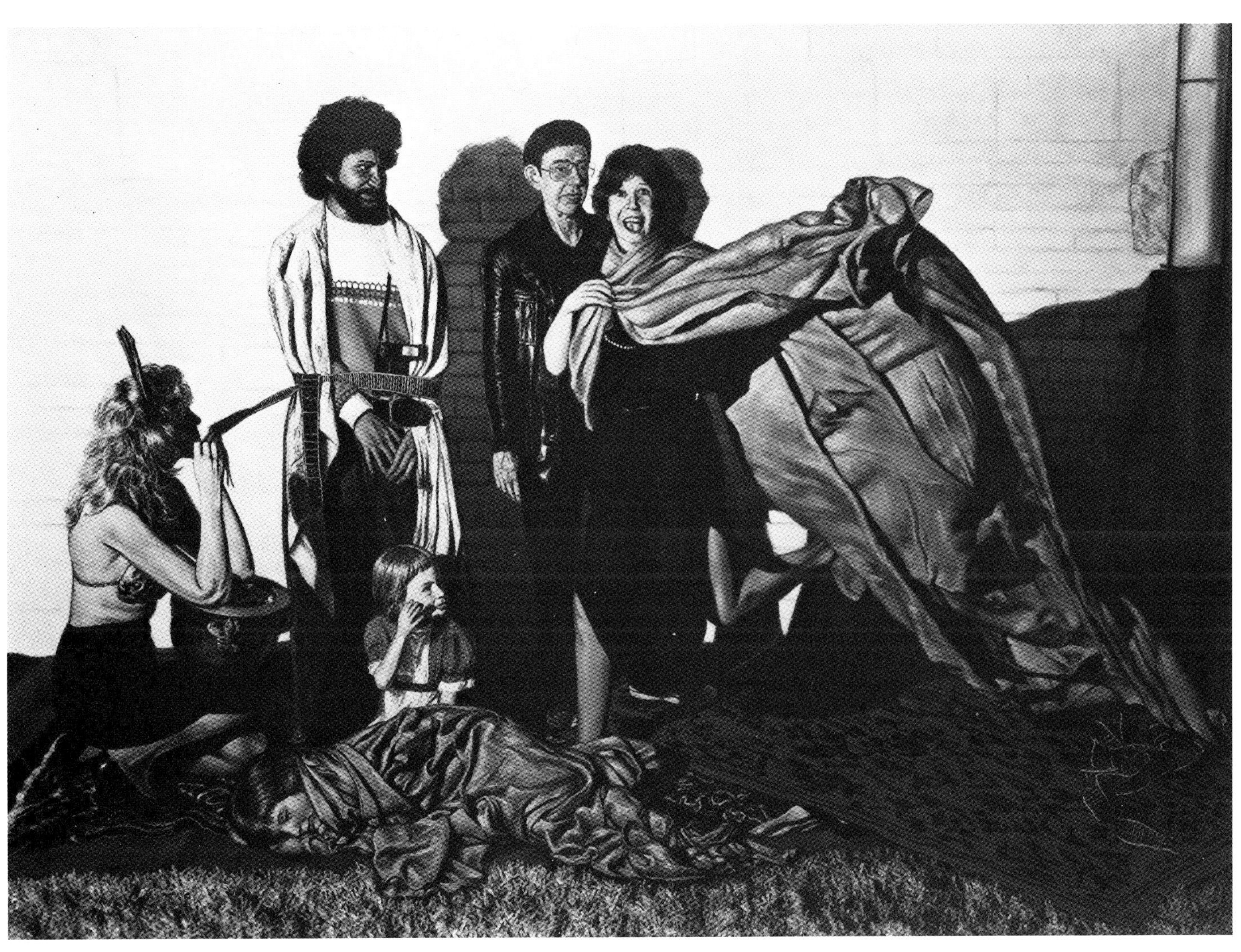

March 25th, #1 1983
Oil on canvas
60 × 84"
Courtesy the artist

Alexa Kleinbard

1952
Born, Abington, Pennsylvania
1974
B.F.A., Philadelphia College of Art,
Pennsylvania

The artist lives and works in Havana,
Florida.

Awards

1979
Individual Artists' Fellowship,
National Endowment for the Arts

Selected Solo Exhibitions

1978
Eyes Gallery, Philadelphia, Pennsylvania
1979-1980
Eric Makler Gallery, Philadelphia,
Pennsylvania
1980
Alexa Kleinbard, University of
South Florida, Tampa
Miami-Dade Junior College, Florida
1981
Third Street Gallery, Atlanta, Georgia

Selected Group Exhibitions

1974
4 Sculptors Show, Philadelphia College of
Art, Pennsylvania
1975
Young Talent, Marian Locks Gallery,
Philadelphia, Pennsylvania
1976
Philadelphia College of Art, Pennsylvania
1977
45th Southeastern, Southeast Center for
Contemporary Art, Winston-Salem, North
Carolina
1978
Forest Avenue Consortium, Atlanta,
Georgia
Outside New York, The New Museum,
New York City
Southeast Center for Contemporary Art,
Winston-Salem, North Carolina
1979
Material Pleasures, Institute for
Contemporary Art, University of
Pennsylvania, Philadelphia
Miniatures, Lawndale Annex, University
of Houston, Texas
1980
Couples, Fendrick Gallery, Washington,
D.C.
1981
Eve Arman Gallery, New York City
Figuratively Sculpting, Institute for Art
and Urban Resources, P.S. 1,
Long Island City, New York
Hodgell Hartman Gallery, Sarasota,
Florida
*The Image of the House in Contemporary
Art,* Lawndale Annex, University of
Houston, Texas

1982
*Art Materialized, Selections from the
Fabric Workshop,* organized by
Independent Curators Incorporated,
New York City (circulated).
Griffith Gallery, Coral Gables, Florida
1983
1983 New Orleans Triennial, New
Orleans Museum of Art, Louisiana

Selected Publications

University of South Florida, Tampa. *Alexa
Kleinbard,* Apr. 10-May 2, 1980. Essay by
Richard Flood. Statement by the artist.

Lawndale Annex, University of Houston,
Texas. *The Image of the House in
Contemporary Art,* Nov. 8-Dec 4, 1981.
Foreword by Charmaine Locke. Essay by
William Simon.

Independent Curators Incorporated, New
York City, *Art Materialized, Selections
from the Fabric Workshop,* 1981. Introduction by Michael A. Quigley. Essays by
Sarah McFadden and Carter Ratcliff.

New Orleans Museum of Art, Louisiana.
1983 New Orleans Triennial, Apr. 8-May
22, 1983. Introduction by William A.
Fagaly. Essay by Linda L. Cathcart.

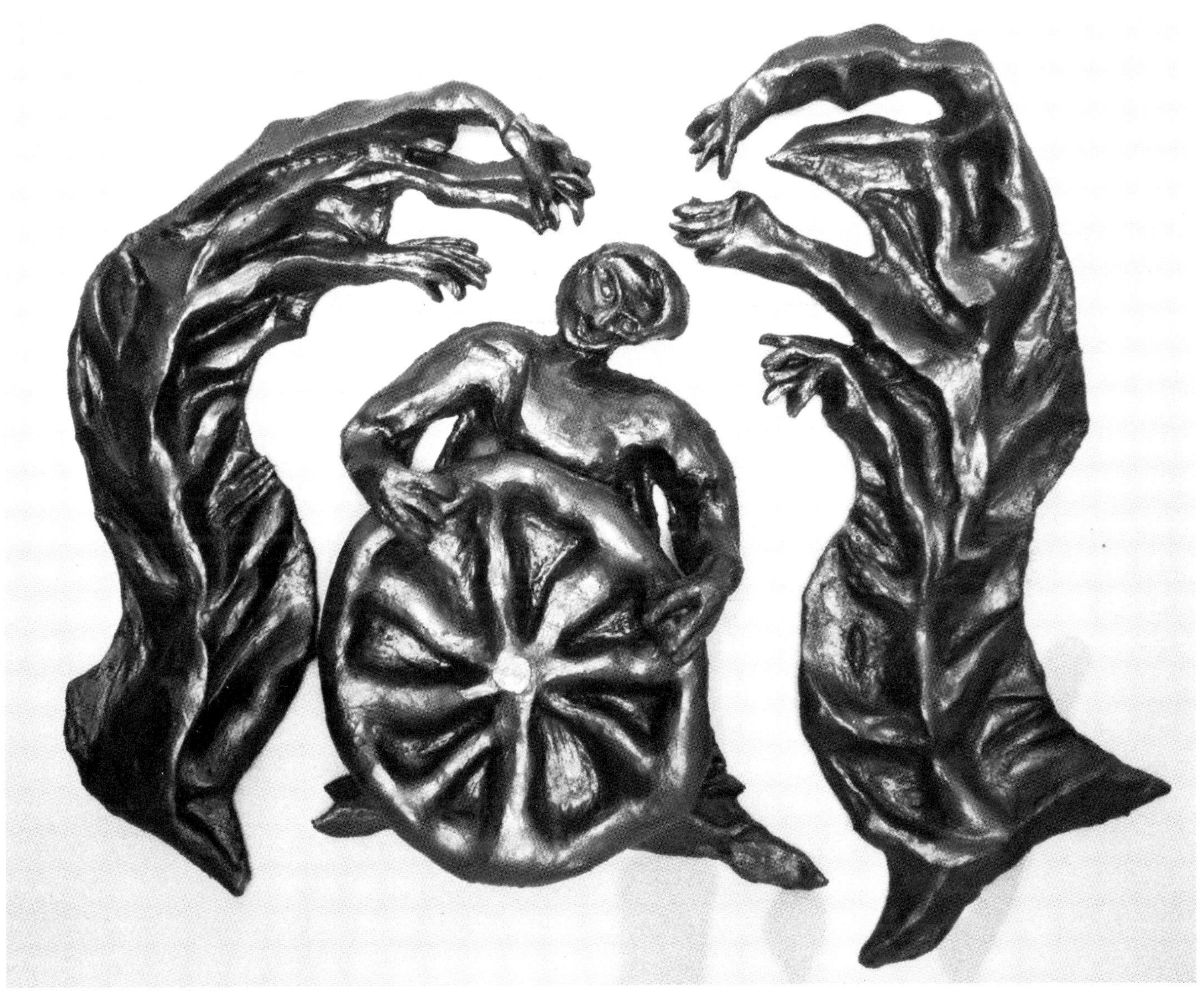

Spinning Wheel 1982
Celluclay, rhoplex, screen, wood and
acrylic
72 × 102 × 16"
Courtesy the artist

Clarence John Laughlin

1905
Born, Lake Charles, Louisiana

The artist began his photographic career in 1934. He lives and works in New Orleans, Louisiana.

Selected Solo Exhibitions

1936
Isaac Delgado Museum of Art, New Orleans, Louisiana
1939
University Art Gallery, Princeton University, New Jersey
1942
New School for Social Research, New York City
1946
The Camera as a Third Eye, Philadelphia, Pennsylvania (circulated)
Walker Art Center, Minneapolis, Minnesota
1948
Ghosts Along the Mississippi, Phillips Collection, Washington, D.C.
San Francisco Museum of Art, California
1949
Northwestern University, Evanston, Illinois
1950
Massachusetts Institute of Technology, Cambridge, Massachusetts
1951
Stanford University, Palo Alto, California
1952
The Art Institute of Chicago, Illinois
1953
Louisiana Plantation Photos, United States Department of State (circulated in Germany)
1954
Cleveland Museum of Art, Ohio
1956
Wadsworth Atheneum, Hartford, Connecticut

1957
The Bronze Age to Brancusi, The Detroit Institute of Arts, Michigan (circulated)
Los Angeles County Museum of Art, California
1965
Old Milwaukee Rediscovered, Milwaukee Public Museum, Wisconsin (circulated)
1967
Phoenix Re-Arisen, Carson Pirie Scott Auditorium, Chicago, Illinois (circulated)
1968
Clarence John Laughlin, Photographs of Victorian Chicago, The Corcoran Gallery of Art, Washington, D.C.
1973
New Orleans Museum of Art, Louisiana
The Personal Eye, The Alfred Stieglitz Center of the Philadelphia Museum of Art, Pennsylvania
1976
Chicago Center for Contemporary Photography, Illinois
Minneapolis Institute of Arts, Minnesota
1978
Daniel Wolf Gallery, New York City
1979
Cronin Gallery, Houston, Texas
1980
Louisiana Plantations, University Library, Tulane University, New Orleans, Louisiana

Selected Group Exhibitions

1940
Julian Levy Gallery, New York City
1949
Mississippi Panorama, The Saint Louis Art Museum, Missouri
1955
4 Photographers: Abbot, Atget, Laughlin, Stieglitz, Yale University, New Haven, Connecticut
1959
Photographer's Choice, Indiana University, Bloomington
Photography at Mid-Century, International Museum of Photography at George Eastman House, Rochester, New York (circulated)

1961
Salon Internationale du Portrait Photographique, Bibliotheque Nationale, Paris, France
1962
Subjektive Fotografie 2, Cologne, West Germany (circulated)
1976
American Photography: Past into Present, Seattle Art Museum, Washington
Photographs from the Julien Levy Collection, Starting with Atget, The Art Institute of Chicago, Illinois
1977
Concerning Photography, The Photographers' Gallery, London, England
1978
40 American Photographers, E. B. Crocker Art Gallery, Sacramento, California

Selected References

The Corcoran Gallery of Art, Washington, D.C. *Clarence John Laughlin, Photographs of Victorian Chicago,* Mar. 2-Apr. 14, 1968. Essay by Rosemary Jones.

The Alfred Stieglitz Center of the Philadelphia Museum of Art, Pennsylvania. *Clarence John Laughlin, The Personal Eye,* Nov. 8, 1973-Jan. 6, 1974. Introduction by Jonathan Williams. Stories by Lafcadio Hearn.

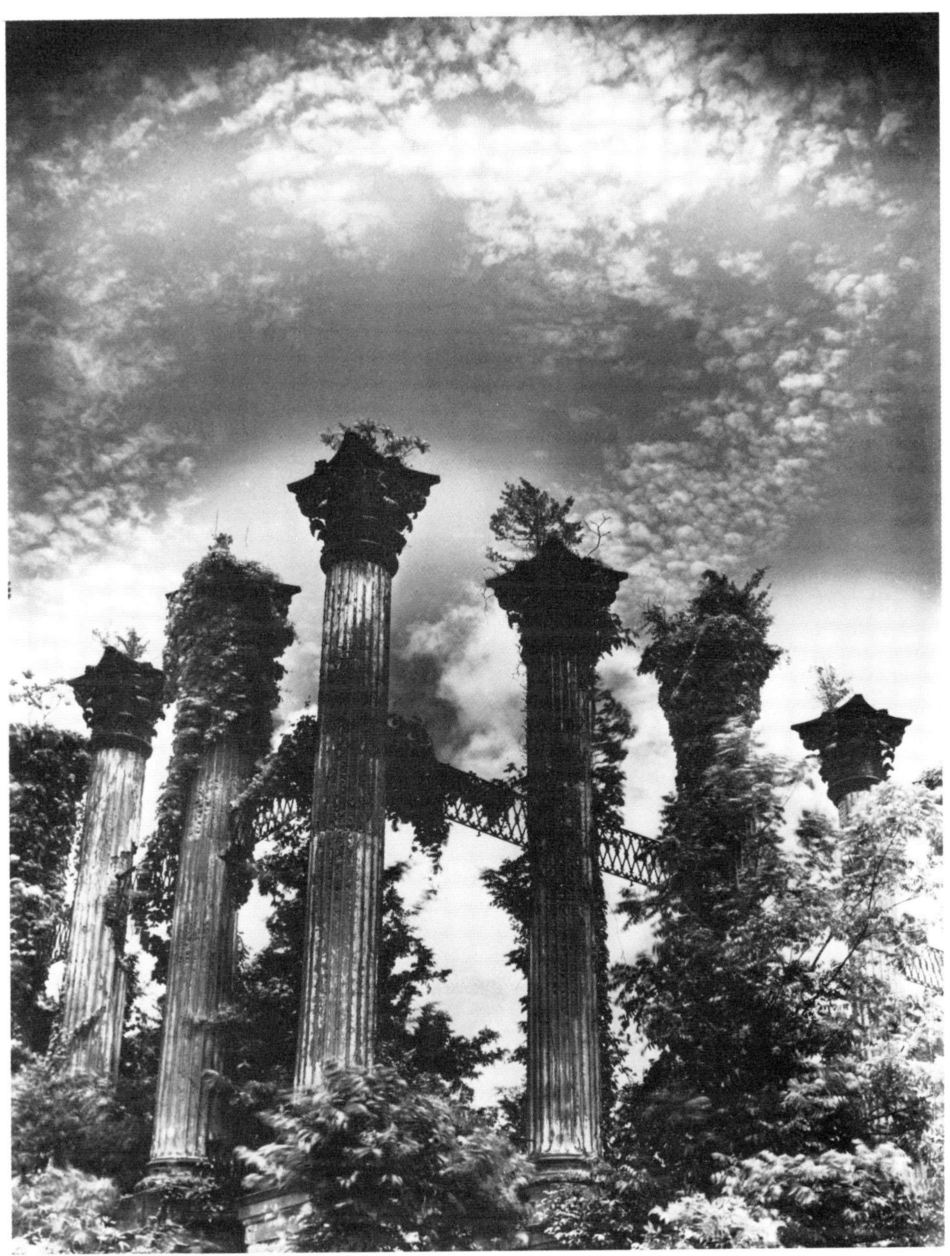

© 1941 Clarence John Laughlin

The Enigma 1941
Gelatin silver print
14 × 10³/₄″
Collection Helen and Rick Gardner,
Houston, Texas

Windsor Plantation, near Port Gibson,
Mississippi, was nearly destroyed during
the course of the Civil War, but survived
only to be destroyed by a fire of unknown
origin in the 1890s. Here, the clouds hang
like a question mark over the mystery of
the ruins, whose tremendous plastered
brick columns are crowned by huge
cast-iron capitals. From the cores of the
brick columns young trees sprout, the
whole structure suggesting an incredible
upsurge of Classical civilization, some-
how completely lost in time and space.

Clarence John Laughlin

Ken Dawson Little

1947
Born, Canyon, Texas
1970
B.F.A., Texas Technical University, Lubbock
1972
M.F.A., University of Utah, Salt Lake City

The artist has taught at several universities including the University of South Florida, Tampa, and University of Montana, Missoula. He has been an associate professor of Art at the University of Oklahoma, Norman since 1980. He lives and works in Norman.

Awards

1977
Individual Craftsmans' Fellowship, Western States Arts Foundation
1982
Individual Artists' Fellowship, National Endowment for the Arts

Selected Solo Exhibitions

1972
University of South Florida, Tampa
1973
Valencia Community College, Orlando, Florida
1975
Montana State University, Bozeman
1976
Gallery of Visual Arts, University of Montana, Missoula
1979
Eastern Washington State University, Cheney
1980
Quay Gallery, San Francisco, California
1983
Quay Gallery, San Francisco, California (circulated)

Selected Group Exhibitions

1971
First Southwestern Exhibition, American Crafts Council Gallery, New York City
1972
Fairtree Gallery, New York City
1974
Tampa Bay Art Center, Florida
1975
National Invitational Exhibition, University Art Gallery, University of Colorado, Boulder
1976
Ceramic Conjunction, Long Beach Museum of Art, California
Land, John Michael Kohler Arts Center, Sheboygan, Wisconsin
1977
Contemporary Ceramic Sculpture, William Hayes Acklund Memorial Art Center, Chapel Hill, North Carolina
1978
Contemporary Crafts, Western States Arts Foundation Fellowship Exhibition (circulated)
1979
Large-Scale Ceramic Sculpture, Nelson Gallery, University of California, Davis
100 Years of American Ceramics, Everson Museum of Art, Syracuse, New York
1981
Animal Images, Renwick Gallery of the Smithsonian Institution, Washington, D.C.
Haystack Benefit Exhibition, Cooper Lynn Gallery, New York City
The Image of the House in Contemporary Art, Lawndale Annex, University of Houston, Texas
Inside/Out: The Self Beyond Likeness, Newport Harbor Art Museum, Newport Beach, California (circulated)
Paint on Clay, John Michael Kohler Arts Center, Sheboygan, Wisconsin

1982
First Annual Wild West Show, Art Gallery, Alberta College of Art, Calgary, Canada
The Lawndale Competition, Lawndale Annex, University of Houston, Texas
Pets and Beasts, Trans America Pyramid Building, San Francisco, California
1983
Winterworks, Oklahoma Art Center, Oklahoma City

Selected References

Newport Harbor Art Museum, Newport Beach, California. *Inside/Out: The Self Beyond Likeness,* May 22-July 12, 1981. Preface by Cathleen S. Gallander. Essays by Lynn Gamwell and Victoria Kogan.

Lawndale Annex, University of Houston, Texas. *The Image of the House in Contemporary Art,* Nov. 8-Dec. 4, 1981. Foreword by Charmaine Locke. Essay by William Simon.

Renwick Gallery of the Smithsonian Institution, Washington, D.C. *Animal Images,* Mar. 13-Aug. 30, 1981. Foreword by Joshua C. Taylor. Essay by Michael W. Monroe.

Quay Gallery, San Francisco, California and participating institutions. *Ken Dawson Little Catalogue of Works, 1983.* Essay by Susan Havens Caldwell.

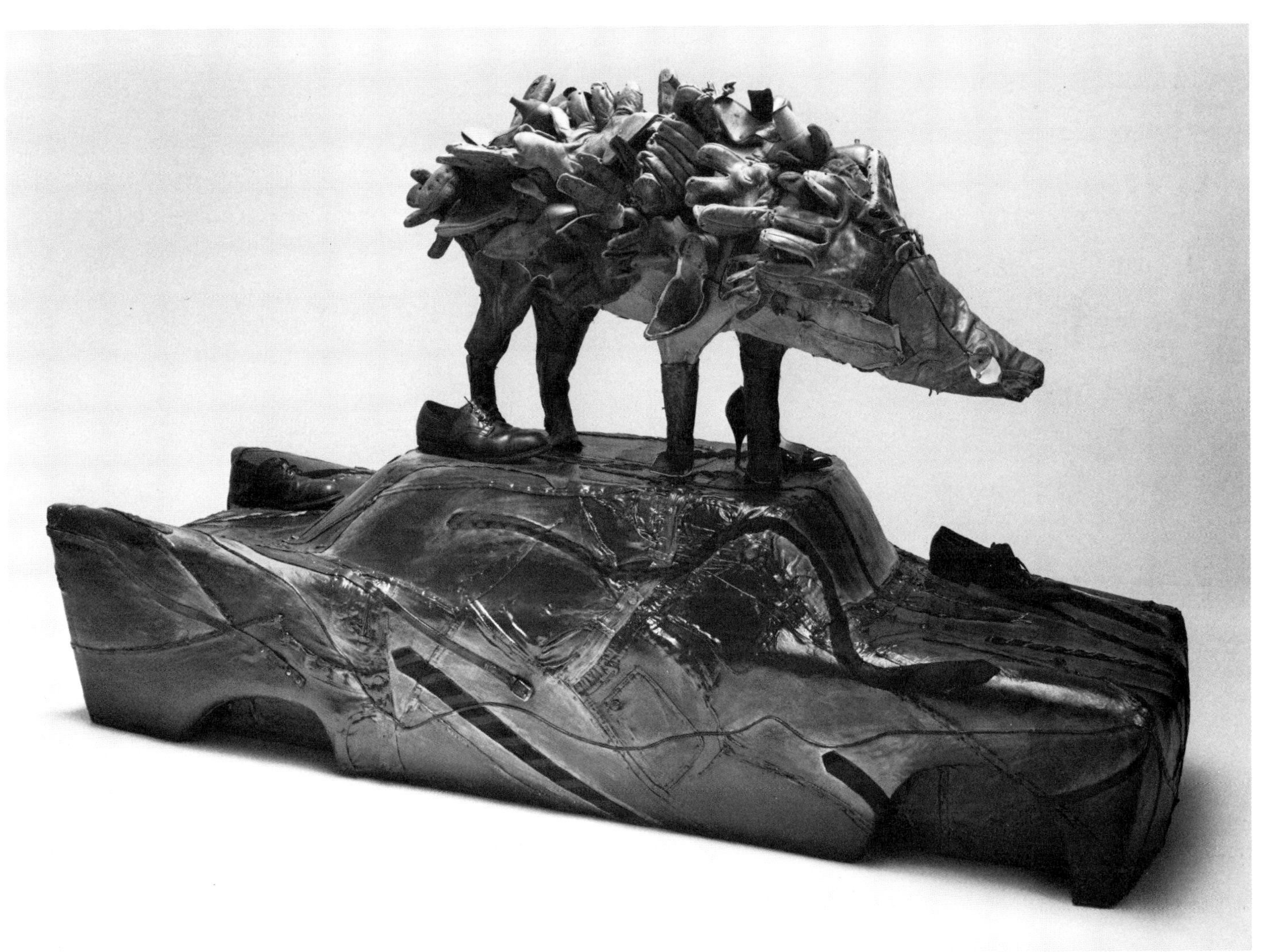

Fury 1983
Mixed media
56 × 90 × 31"
Courtesy the artist

Ed McGowin

1938
Born, Hattiesburg, Mississippi
1961
B.S., University of Southern Mississippi,
Hattiesburg
1964
M.A., University of Alabama, Tuscaloosa

The artist has taught at the Corcoran
School of Art in Washington, D.C.
McGowin assumed a professorship at the
State University of New York at Old
Westbury in 1978 and became chairman
of the Art Department in 1979. He lives
and works in New York City.

Awards

1967, 1976, 1980
Individual Artists' Fellowship,
National Endowment for the Arts
1972
Cassandra Foundation Grant

Selected Solo Exhibitions

1962
The Corcoran Gallery of Art,
Washington, D.C.
1967
Henri Gallery, Washington, D.C.
1968
Martha Jackson Gallery, New York City
1971
Galerie Simonne Stern, New Orleans,
Louisiana
1972
The Baltimore Museum of Art, Maryland
Pyramid Galleries, Ltd., Washington, D.C.
1974
Pyramid Galleries, Ltd., Washington, D.C.
1975
Ed McGowin's True Stories, The Corcoran
Gallery of Art, Washington, D.C.
(circulated)
Galerie Simonne Stern,
New Orleans, Louisiana
1977
Fendrick Gallery, Washington, D.C.
1978
Iolas Gallery, New York City
1980
Fendrick Gallery, Washington, D.C.

1982
Iolas/Jackson Gallery, New York City
1983
Institute for Art and Urban Resources,
P.S.1, Long Island City,
New York
Time Inscape, Graduate School of Design,
Harvard University, Cambridge,
Massachusetts

Selected Group Exhibitions

1966
*Annual Exhibition of Contemporary
Sculpture and Prints,* Whitney Museum of
American Art, New York City
1967
New Acquisitions Exhibition, Whitney
Museum of American Art, New York City
1968
*Annual Exhibition of Contemporary
American Sculpture,* Whitney Museum of
American Art, New York City
Art in Washington, Washington Gallery of
Modern Art, Washington, D.C.
1969
Gilliam, Krebs, McGowin, The Corcoran
Gallery of Art, Washington, D.C.
A Plastic Presence, The Jewish Museum,
New York City
1970
Washington: 20 Years, The Baltimore
Museum of Art, Maryland
1974
Painting and Sculpture Today 1974, The
Contemporary Art Society of the
Indianapolis Museum of Art, Indiana
(circulated)
1975
Gulf Coast, East Coast, West Coast,
Contemporary Arts Museum, Houston,
Texas
1976
Artists/Poets, Washington Project for the
Arts, Washington, D.C.
*Private Notations: Artists's Sketchbooks
II,* Philadelphia College of Art,
Pennsylvania
1977
American Narrative/Story Art: 1967-77,
Contemporary Arts Museum, Houston,
Texas (circulated)

1978
Art on the Beach, Creative Time, Inc.
New York City
*The Sense of Self: From Self Portrait to
Autobiography,* Neuberger Museum,
State University of New York at Purchase
1981
*The Image of the House in Contemporary
Art,* Lawndale Annex, University of
Houston, Texas
*The Southern Voice: Terry Allen, Vernon
Fisher, Ed McGowin,* Fort Worth Art
Museum, Texas
1982
Mayor Byrne's Mile of Sculpture,
Chicago, Illinois
1983
*Space Framed II: Work by Contemporary
Sculptors,* Graduate School of Design,
Harvard University, Cambridge,
Massachusetts

Selected References

Contemporary Arts Museum, Houston,
Texas. *American Narrative/Story Art:
1967-77,* Dec. 17, 1977-Feb. 25, 1978.
Preface by James Harithas. Introduction
by Paul Schimmel. Essays by Alan
Sondheim and Marc Freidus.

The Corcoran Gallery of Art, Washington,
D.C. *Ed McGowin's True Stories,* Sept.
13-Oct. 26, 1975, Introduction by Roy
Slade. Essay by Jane Livingston. Stories
by Ed McGowin.

Fort Worth Art Museum, Texas. *The
Southern Voice: Terry Allen, Vernon
Fisher, Ed McGowin,* Sept. 13-Oct. 25,
1981. Introduction by Susan Freudenheim.
Essay by Marge Goldwater.

Lawndale Annex, University of Houston,
Texas. *The Image of the House in
Contemporary Art,* Nov. 8-Dec. 4, 1981.
Foreword by Charmaine Locke. Essay by
William Simon.

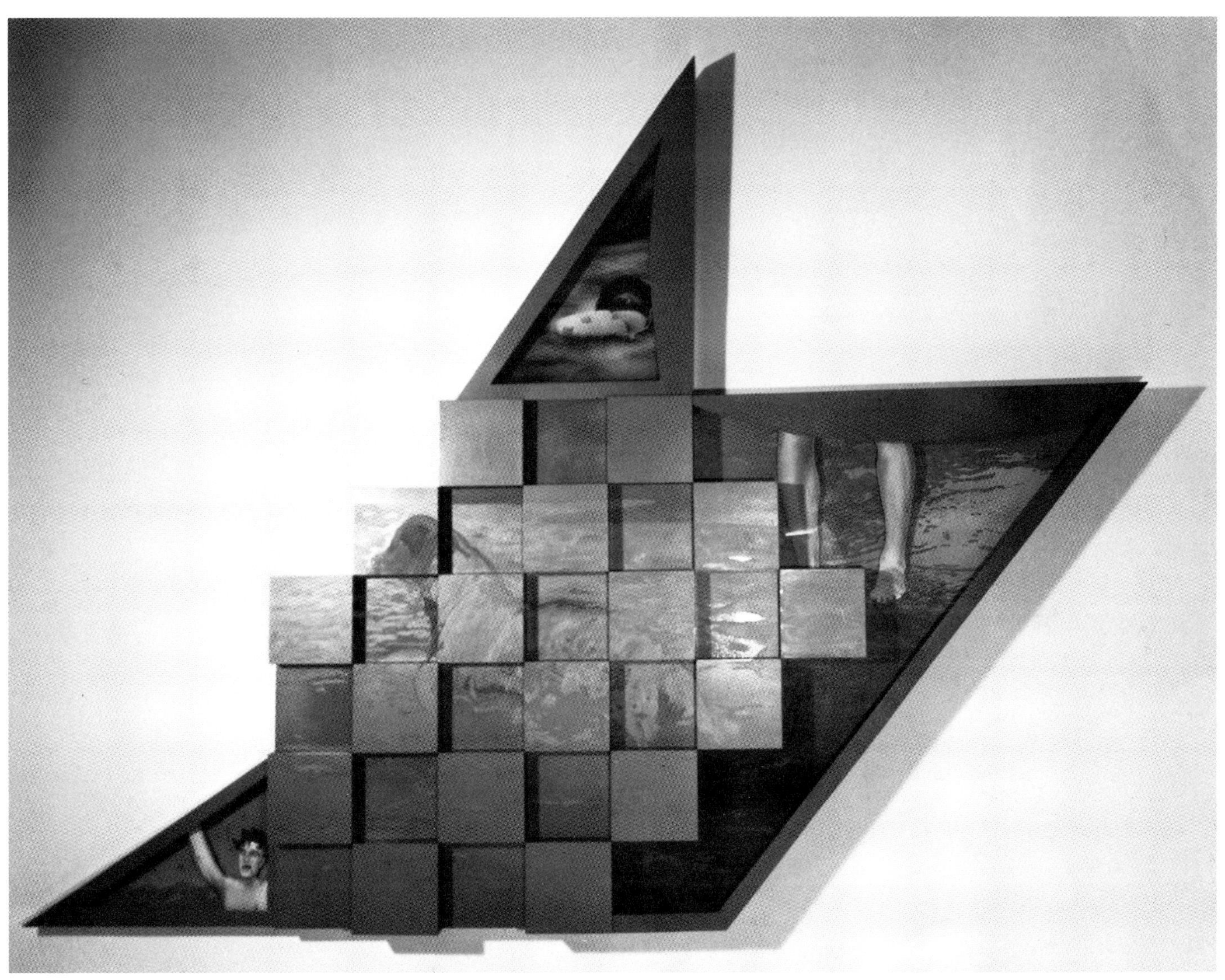

Rescue 1983
Mixed media
120 × 144"
Courtesy the artist and
Iolas/Jackson Gallery,
New York City

Melissa Miller

1951
Born, Houston, Texas
1974
B.F.A., University of New Mexico,
Albuquerque

The artist lives and works in Austin,
Texas.

Awards

1979, 1982
Individual Artists' Fellowship,
National Endowment for the Arts

Selected Solo Exhibitions

1978
Young Texas Artist Series, Amarillo Art
Center, Texas
1981
Art Museum of South Texas,
Corpus Christi
1982
Melissa Miller: Recent Paintings,
Contemporary Arts Museum, Houston,
Texas

Selected Group Exhibitions

1973
Edwards, Jurkowitz, Miller and Wiley,
University of New Mexico, Albuquerque
1974
Southwest Fine Arts Biennial, Museum of
New Mexico, Santa Fe
1977
Painting and Sculpture Exhibition, The
One Seguin Art Center, Texas
Women and Their Work, Laguna Gloria
Art Museum, Austin, Texas
1978
*Austin Contemporary Visual Arts
Association,* St. Edward's University,
Austin, Texas
Works on Paper: Southwest 1978, Dallas
Museum of Fine Arts, Texas

1979
The Amarillo Competition, Amarillo Art
Center, Texas
Austin Contemporary Art Exhibition,
Trinity House Gallery, Austin, Texas
*New Works: Melissa Miller and Claudia
Reese,* Laguna Gloria at First Federal,
Austin, Texas
Woman-in-Sight: New Art in Texas,
(organized by Women and Their Work),
Dougherty Cultural Arts Center, Austin,
Texas
Vital Signs, Aperture Gallery, Austin,
Texas
1980
Introductions '80, T.V. Robinson Gallery,
Houston, Texas
Invitational '80, Longview Museum and
Art Center, Texas
1980 New Orleans Triennial, New
Orleans Museum of Art, Louisiana
Texas Only, Laguna Gloria Art Museum,
Austin, Texas
Visions and Figurations, The Art Gallery,
California State University, Fullerton
1981
Wendy Edwards and Melissa Miller,
Mattingly Baker Gallery, Dallas, Texas
1982
New Works, Summer 1982, Laguna Gloria
Art Museum, Austin, Texas
Patrick Gallery, Austin, Texas
1983
New Figurative Drawing in Texas, San
Antonio Art Institute, Texas
1983 Biennial Exhibition, Whitney
Museum of American Art, New York City
Images of Texas, Archer M. Huntington
Gallery, University Art Museum, The
University of Texas at Austin (circulated)

Selected References

New Orleans Museum of Art, Louisiana.
1980 New Orleans Triennial, Oct. 3-Nov.
16, 1980. Introduction by William A.
Fagaly. Essay by Marcia Tucker.

Contemporary Arts Museum, Houston,
Texas. *Melissa Miller: Recent Paintings,*
Dec. 19, 1981-Jan. 24, 1982. Essay by
Linda L. Cathcart.

The Art Gallery, California State
University, Fullerton. *Visions and
Figurations,* Nov. 7-Dec. 11, 1980.
Foreword by Dextra Frankel. Essay by
Ron Faulds.

Whitney Museum of American Art, New
York City. *1983 Biennial Exhibition,* Mar.
15-May 22, 1983. Foreword by Tom
Armstrong. Preface by John G. Hanardt,
Barbara Haskell, Richard Marshall and
Patterson Sims.

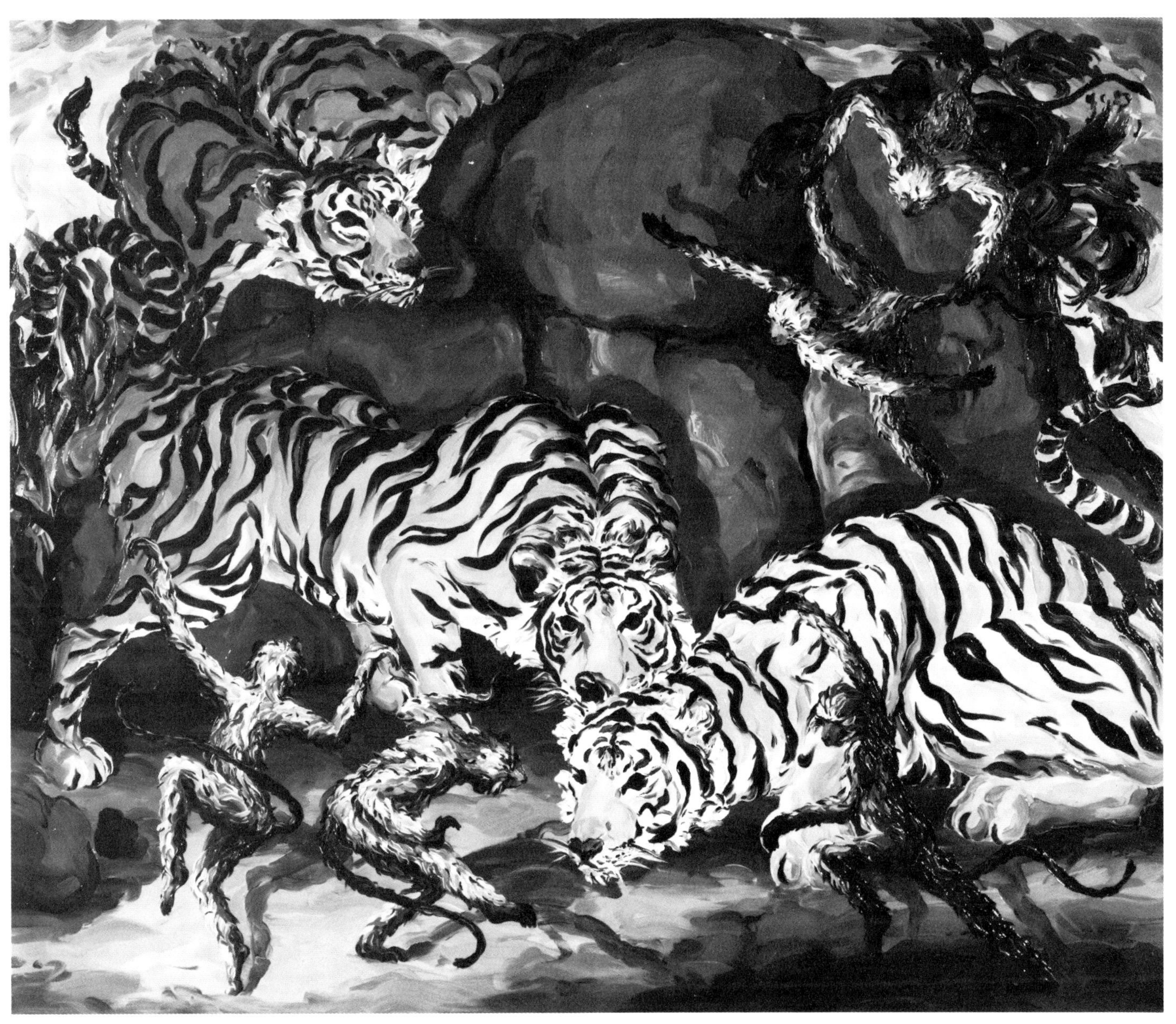

Untitled (Tigers) 1982
Oil on canvas
58 × 70"
Collection Bob Wilson, Houston, Texas

Nic Nicosia

1951
Born, Dallas, Texas
1974
B.A., North Texas State University, Denton

The artist lives and works in Dallas, Texas.

Selected Solo Exhibitions

1978
White Mule Gallery, Denton, Texas
1981
Brown Lupton Gallery, Texas Christian University, Fort Worth
1982
Artists Space, New York City
Nic Nicosia/Domestic Dramas, Delahunty Gallery, Dallas, Texas
1983
Light Song Gallery, University of Arizona, Tucson

Selected Group Exhibitions

1978
Self-Portrait International, Northlight Gallery, Arizona State University, Tempe
1980
Texas Only, Laguna Gloria Art Museum, Austin, Texas
1981
American Vision, New York University, New York City
Invitational '81, Longview Museum and Arts Center, Texas
New Photographics '81, Central Washington State University, Ellensburg
The New Photography, Contemporary Arts Museum, Houston, Texas
Photoworks: Steve Dennie/Nic Nicosia, 500 Exposition Gallery, Dallas, Texas
Staged Shots, Delahunty Gallery, Dallas, Texas
Steve Dennie/Nic Nicosia, Galveston Arts Center on the Strand, Texas
Texas Photo Sampler, Washington Project for the Arts, Washington, D.C. (circulated)
1982
Beyond Photography: The Fabricated Image, Delahunty Gallery, New York City
Fabricated Images/Color Photography, Magnuson-Lee Gallery, Boston, Massachusetts
HALLWALLS, Buffalo, New York
Henrich, Nicosia, Williams, Texas Gallery, Houston
Space Framed I, Graduate School of Design, Harvard University, Cambridge, Massachusetts

1983
Image Fabrique, Musee Nationale d'Art Moderne, Centre National d'Art et de Culture Georges Pompidou, Paris, France
1983 New Orleans Triennial, New Orleans Museum of Art, Louisiana
3-D Photographs, Castelli Graphics, New York City
Touch with Your Eyes, Feel with Your Mind: Surfaces in Contemporary Art, Laguna Gloria Art Museum, Austin, Texas
1983 Biennial Exhibition, Whitney Museum of American Art, New York City

Selected References

Washington Project for the Arts, Washington, D.C. *Texas Photo Sampler,* Jan. 6-31, 1981. Introduction by Al Nodal. Essay by Ed Hill.

Contemporary Arts Museum, Houston, Texas. *The New Photography,* Jan. 7-Feb. 22, 1981. Essays by Linda L. Cathcart and Marti Mayo.

New Orleans Museum of Art, Louisiana. *1983 New Orleans Triennial,* Apr. 8-May 22, 1983. Introduction by William A. Fagaly. Essay by Linda L. Cathcart.

Whitney Museum of American Art, New York City. *1983 Biennial Exhibition,* Mar. 15-May 22, 1983. Foreword by Tom Armstrong. Preface by John G. Hanhardt, Barbara Haskell, Richard Marshall and Patterson Sims.

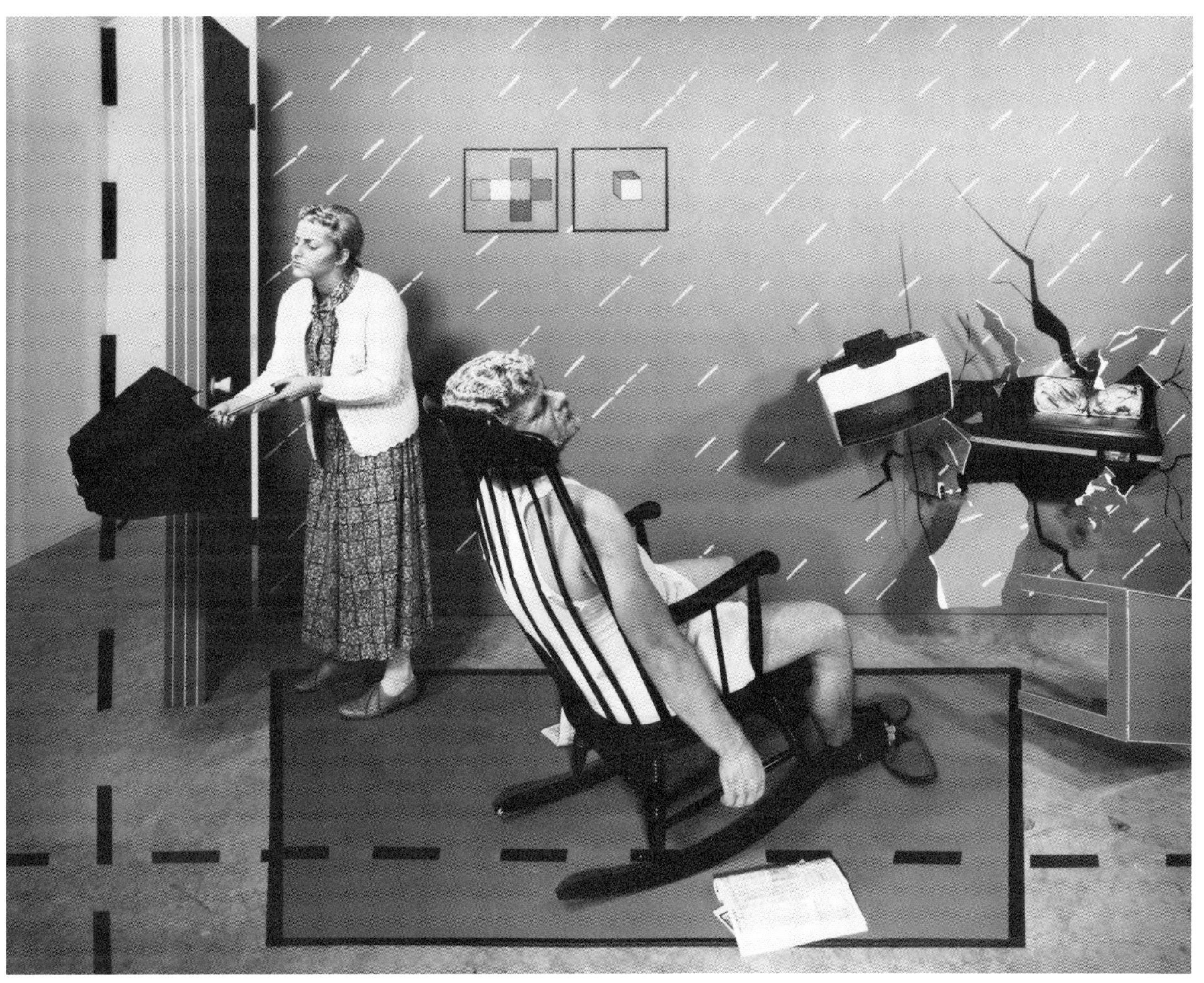

*Domestic Drama #7 (Near Modern
Disaster #1)* 1982
Cibachrome print
40 × 50″
Collection Steve Dennie, Dallas, Texas

Francie Rich

1947
Born, Minneapolis, Minnesota
1969
B.F.A., Minneapolis College of Art and Design, Minnesota
1970
M.F.A., California College of Arts and Crafts, Oakland

The artist has taught at several universities. Since 1976, she has been an associate professor at St. Mary's Dominican College in New Orleans. She lives and works in Covington, Louisiana.

Awards

1971
Artist-in-Residence Fellowship Grant, Roswell Museum Art Center, New Mexico

Selected Solo Exhibitions

1969
Minneapolis Art Institute, Minnesota (circulated)
1972
Whatcom Museum of History and Art, Bellingham, Washington
1973
Roswell Museum and Art Center, New Mexico
1974
Circle Graphics, New Orleans, Louisiana
1977
Mixed Media, Newspace Gallery, New Orleans, Louisiana
1979
University of New Orleans, Louisiana
1980
Weddings, Galerie Simonne Stern, New Orleans, Louisiana

Selected Group Exhibitions

1969
Young American Exhibition, Ben and Abbey Gray Foundation, St. Paul, Minnesota, and the Smithsonian Institution, Washington, D.C. (circulated in India and Iran)
1969-1976
118: An Art Gallery, Minneapolis, Minnesota
1971-1973
Gorner and Millard Gallery, London, England
Atrium Orbis Gallery, Santa Fe, New Mexico
1972
The World Through Art, Ben and Abbey Gray Foundation, St. Paul, Minnesota
1973
New Orleans Museum of Art, Louisiana
1974
Downtown Gallery, New Orleans, Louisiana
1975
X-Rated America, Photo Exchange Gallery, New Orleans, Louisiana
1977
1977 Artists Biennial, New Orleans Museum of Art, Louisiana
1978
Animal Fantasies, Contemporary Arts Center, New Orleans, Louisiana
1979
Animals: Celebration and Communion, Sonoma State University, California
Miniatures, Lawndale Annex, University of Houston, Texas
Seven Artists from Louisiana, University of West Florida, Pensacola
1980-1982
Art for Arts' Sake, Contemporary Arts Center, New Orleans, Louisiana
1980
Louisiana Miniatures, Contemporary Arts Center, New Orleans, Louisiana
1981
Galerie De Villa, New Orleans, Louisiana

1982
Art Cars, Institute for Art and Urban Resources, P.S. 1, Long Island City, New York
Brother Michael, Contemporary Arts Center, New Orleans, Louisiana
Women's Week Art Exhibition, St. Mary's Dominican College, New Orleans, Louisiana
1983
Dog Show, Galerie Jules LaForge, New Orleans, Louisiana
Elmhurst Park Gallery, Lafayette, Louisiana
1983 New Orleans Triennial, New Orleans Museum of Art, Louisiana

Selected References

New Orleans Museum of Art, Louisiana. *1977 Artists Biennial,* May 28-July 3, 1977. Introduction by William A. Fagaly. Essay by Jack Boulton.

New Orleans Museum of Art, Louisiana. *1983 New Orleans Triennial,* Apr. 8-May 22, 1983. Introduction by William A. Fagaly. Essay by Linda L. Cathcart.

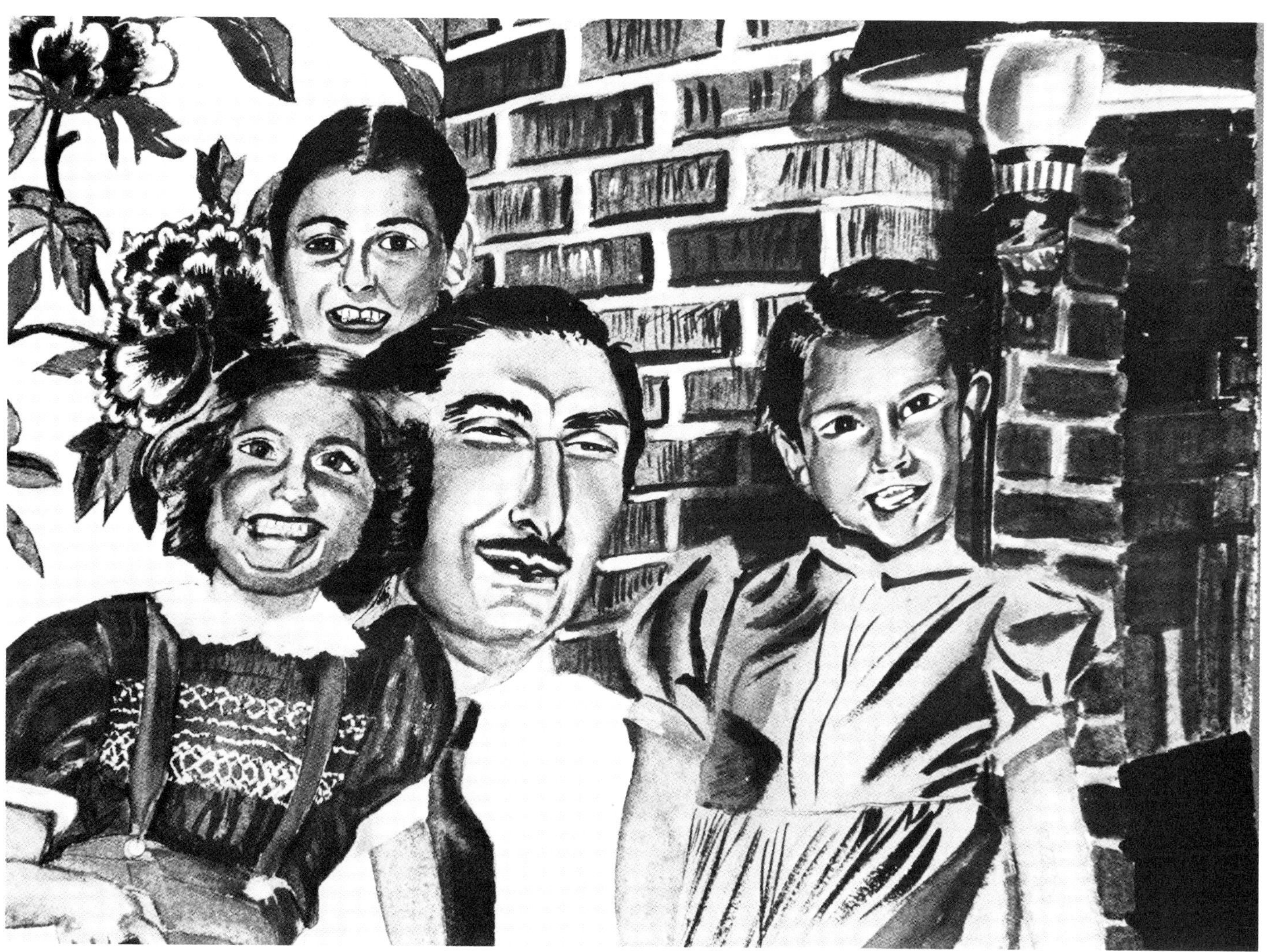

Used Car Salesman and His Daughters
1980-1982
Gouache on paper
13½ × 17″
Courtesy the artist

Art Rosenbaum

1938
Born, Ogdensburgh, New York
1960
B.A., Columbia University, New York City
1961
M.F.A., Columbia University,
New York City

The artist has taught at several
universities. Since 1976 he has been
an associate professor of Art, University
of Georgia, Athens. He lives and works
in Athens.

Awards

1964
Fulbright Grant
1979
Folk Arts Grant,
National Endowment for the Arts

Selected Solo Exhibitions

1963
Columbia University, New York City
1970
Davenport Municipal Gallery, Iowa
Cedar Rapids Art Center, Iowa
1974
Razor Gallery, New York City
1977
Razor Gallery, New York City
1978
Skydome Gallery, Lexington, Kentucky
1981
Anton Gallery, Washington, D.C.

Selected Group Exhibitions

1954
Fifty Indiana Prints, Herron Museum,
Indianapolis, Indiana
1955-1957
Indiana Artists, Herron Museum,
Indianapolis, Indiana
1958
Fifty Indiana Prints, Herron Museum,
Indianapolis, Indiana
1960
Fifty Indiana Prints, Herron Museum,
Indianapolis, Indiana
1967
Indiana Artists, Herron Museum,
Indianapolis, Indiana
1972
Iowa Artists Annual, Des Moines
Art Center
Iowa State University, Ames
Peoria Arts Guild, Illinois
1973
Museum of Art, University of Iowa,
Iowa City
1976
Iowa Artists Annual, Des Moines Art
Center, Iowa
1977
Razor Gallery, New York City
1978
Piedmont Graphics, Greenville County
Museum of Art, Greenville,
South Carolina
Razor Gallery, New York City (circulated)
Springfield Art Museum, Missouri
Viscera, Forest Avenue Consortium,
Atlanta, Georgia

1981
More Land Than Sky, National Museum
of American Art, Smithsonian Institution,
Washington, D.C. (circulated)
1983
1983 New Orleans Triennial, New
Orleans Museum of Art, Louisiana
*What Artists Have to Say About Nuclear
War,* Nexus Gallery, Inc., Atlanta, Georgia

Selected References

National Museum of American Art,
Smithsonian Institution, Washington, D.C.
More Land Than Sky, Oct. 30, 1981-
Jan. 3, 1982. Statement by Harry Lowe.
Text by Barbara Shiffleu Nosanow.

New Orleans Museum of Art, Louisiana.
1983 New Orleans Triennial, Apr. 8-
May 22, 1983. Introduction by William A.
Fagaly. Essay by Linda L. Cathcart.

Nexus Gallery, Inc., Atlanta, Georgia.
*What Artists Have to Say About Nuclear
War,* May 13-June 12, 1983. Essays by
John Houwett, Jeff Kipnis and Chip
Reynolds.

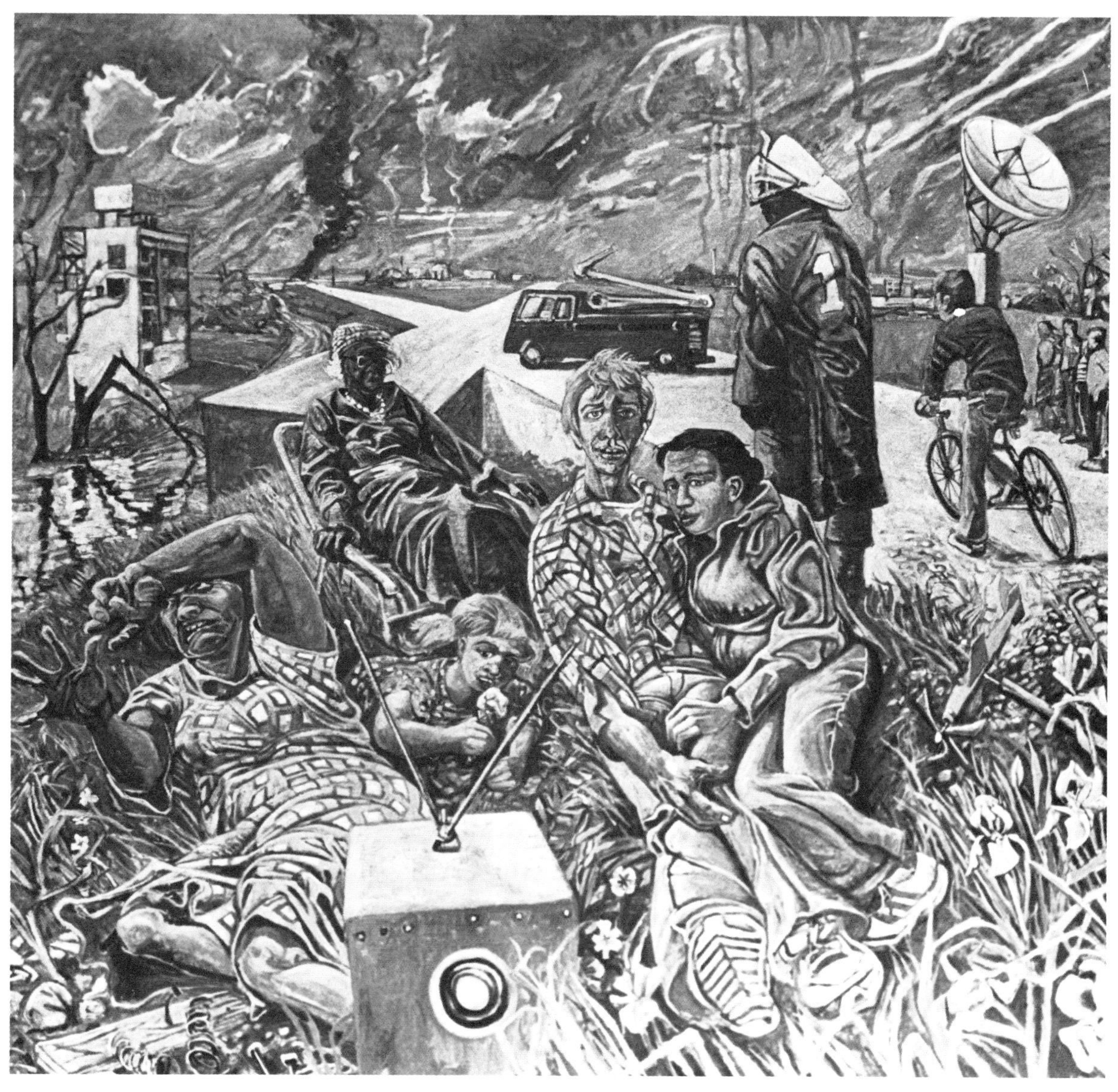

Untitled 1983
Oil and alkyd resin on canvas
60 × 64″
Courtesy the artist

Julian Schnabel

1951
Born, New York City
1972
B.F.A., University of Houston, Texas
1974
Independent Study Program, Whitney Museum of American Art, New York City

The artist lives and works in New York City.

Selected Solo Exhibitions

1976
Contemporary Arts Museum, Houston, Texas
1978
Galerie December, Dusseldorf, West Germany
1979
Daniel Weinberg Gallery, San Francisco, California
Mary Boone Gallery, New York City
1980
Bruno Bischofberger, Zurich, Switzerland
Young/Hoffman Gallery, Chicago, Illinois
1981
Anthony D'Offay Gallery, London, England
Mary Boone Gallery and Leo Castelli Gallery, New York City
1982
Daniel Weinberg Gallery, San Francisco, California
Margo Leavin Gallery, Los Angeles, California
Stedlijk Museum, Amsterdam, the Netherlands
Tate Gallery, London, England
1983
Leo Castelli Gallery, New York City

Selected Group Exhibitions

1971
Hidden Houston, University of St. Thomas, Houston, Texas
1972
Louisiana Gallery, Houston, Texas
1974
W.I.S.P. Exhibition, Whitney Museum of American Art, New York City
1977
Surrogate/Self Portraits, Holly Soloman Gallery, New York City
1979
Four Artists, HALLWALLS, Buffalo, New York
Visionary Images, The Rennaissance Society at The University of Chicago, Illinois
1980
L'Amerique aux Independants, Grand Palais, Paris, France
La Biennale di Venezia, Venice, Italy
Daniel Templon, Paris, France
Drawings, Mary Boone Gallery, New York City
Drawings, Mattingly Baker Gallery, Dallas, Texas
Mary Boone Gallery, New York City
On Paper, Institute of Contemporary Art, Richmond, Virginia
Painting and Sculpture Today, Indianapolis Museum of Art, Indiana
1981
Body Language, Hayden Gallery, Massachusetts Institute of Technology, Cambridge (circulated)
The Contemporary Image, Akron Art Institute, Ohio
1981 Biennial Exhibition, Whitney Museum of American Art, New York City
Schnabel, Rothenberg, Moskowitz, Basel Kunstmuseum, Switzerland (circulated)
Westkunst: Heute, Cologne, West Germany

1982
The Americans: The Collage, Contemporary Arts Museum, Houston, Texas
La Biennale di Venezia, Venice, Italy
Castelli and His Artists, La Jolla Museum of Contemporary Art, California (circulated)
Focus on the Figure, Whitney Museum of American Art, New York City
Issues: New Allegory, Institute of Contemporary Art, Boston, Massachusetts
74th American Exhibition, The Art Institute of Chicago, Illinois
60/80: Attitude, Concepts, Images, Stedlijk Museum, Amsterdam, the Netherlands
1983
Directions 1983, Hirshhorn Museum and Sculpture Garden, Smithsonian Institution, Washington, D.C.

Selected References

Hayden Gallery, Massachusetts Institute of Technology, Cambridge. *Body Language,* Oct. 2-Dec. 24, 1981. Essay by Roberta Smith.

Stedelijk Museum, Amsterdam, the Netherlands. *Julian Schnabel,* Jan. 28-Mar. 3, 1982. Foreword by Edy de Wilde. Essay by Rene Ricard.

Contemporary Arts Museum, Houston, Texas. *The Americans: The Collage,* July 11-Oct. 3, 1982. Foreword and essay by Linda L. Cathcart.

Hirshhorn Museum and Sculpture Garden, Smithsonian Institution, Washington, D.C. *Directions 1983,* Mar. 10-May 15, 1983. Foreword by Abram Lerner. Introduction and essay by Phyllis Rosenzweig.

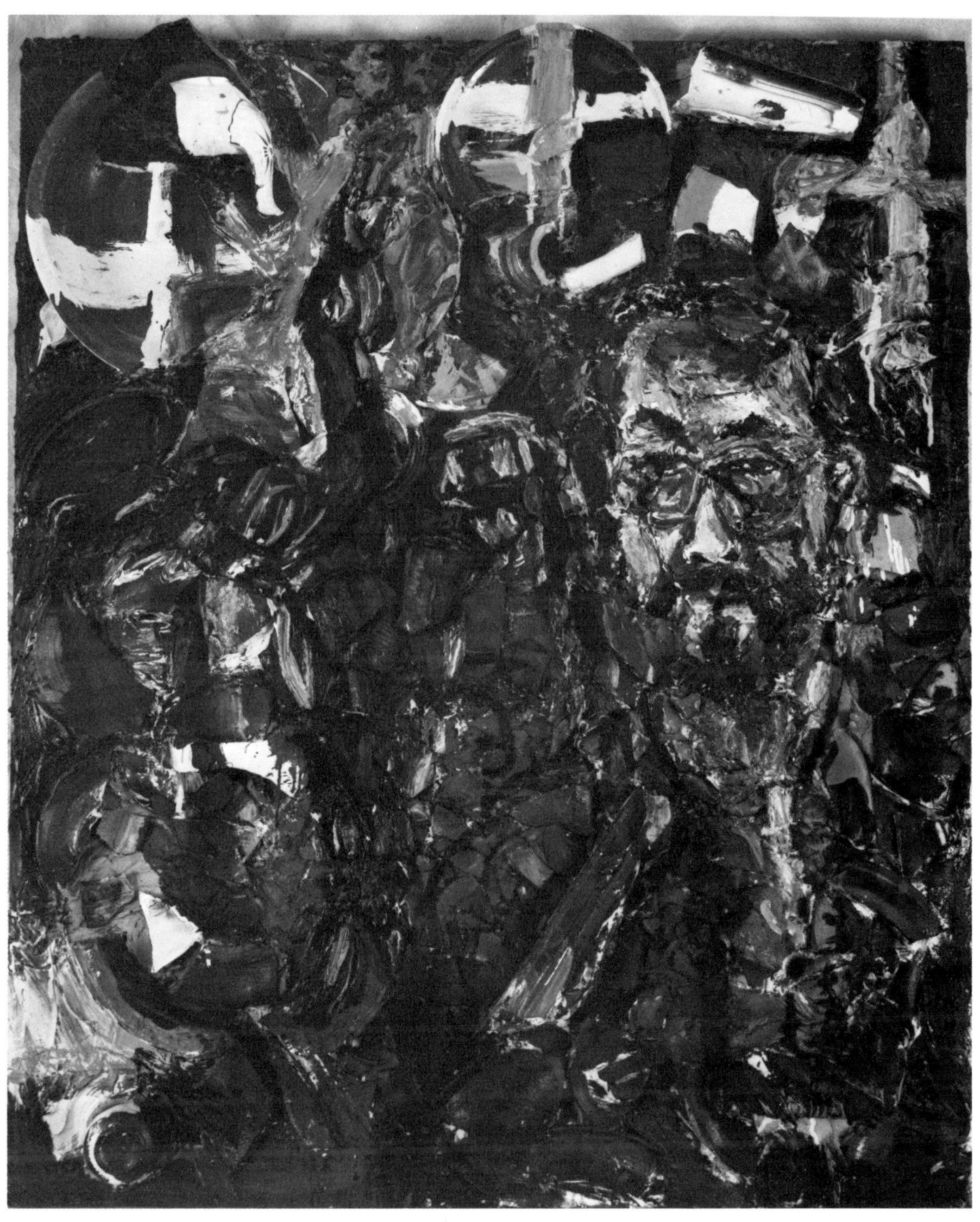

Portrait of Michael Tracy 1983
Oil, plates and bondo on wood
48 × 40″
Collection Michael Tracy,
San Ygnacio, Texas

Lee N. Smith III

1950
Born, New Orleans, Louisiana
1969-1970
Studied, El Centro Junior College, Dallas, Texas

The artist lives and works in Dallas, Texas.

Selected Solo Exhibitions

1978
Eastfield College, Dallas, Texas
1979
Mountain View College, Dallas, Texas
The University of Texas at Arlington
1980
DW Gallery, Dallas, Texas
1981
Focus: Lee N. Smith III, Fort Worth Art Museum, Texas
Texas Christian University, Fort Worth, Texas

Selected Group Exhibitions

1978
8th National Southwest Texas State University Works on Paper Exhibition, Southwest Texas State University, San Marcos
20th Annual Eight State Exhibition of Painting and Sculpture, Oklahoma Art Center, Oklahoma City
Works on Paper: Southwest 1978, Dallas Museum of Fine Arts, Texas

1979
11th Monroe National Art Exhibition, Masur Museum of Art, Monroe, Louisiana
6th Annual Midwestern Printmaking and Drawing Competition, Philbrook Art Center, Tulsa, Oklahoma
1980
Inside Texas Borders, South Texas Artmobile, Corpus Christi State University, Texas
1980 New Orleans Triennial, New Orleans Museum of Art, Louisiana
1981
'81 West Art and the Law, Minnesota Museum of Art, St. Paul
4 Painters: Jones, Stack, Smith, Utterback, Contemporary Arts Museum, Houston, Texas
1982
Fun and Games, The Art Center, Waco, Texas
1982 Biennial National Exhibition, Meadows Museum of Art of Centenary College, Shreveport, Louisiana
Small But Important, Nexus Gallery, Inc., Atlanta, Georgia
1983
'83 Art and Law Invitational, Memorial Arts Center, Atlanta, Georgia
Invitational, Laguna Gloria Art Museum, Austin, Texas
Invitational '83, Longview Museum and Art Center, Texas

Selected References

New Orleans Museum of Art, Louisiana. *1980 New Orleans Triennial,* Oct. 3-Nov. 16, 1980. Introduction by William A. Fagaly. Essay by Marcia Tucker.

Fort Worth Art Museum, Texas. *Focus: Lee N. Smith III,* Feb. 7-Mar. 22, 1981. Essay by Marge Goldwater.

Minnesota Museum of Art, St. Paul. *'81 West Art and the Law,* June 12-July 12, 1981. Foreword by Dean Swanson and James V. Toscano. Introduction by G. L. Cafesjian.

Contemporary Arts Museum, Houston, Texas. *4 Painters: Jones, Stack, Smith, Utterback,* Oct. 10-Nov. 29, 1981. Introduction and essays by Linda L. Cathcart and Marti Mayo.

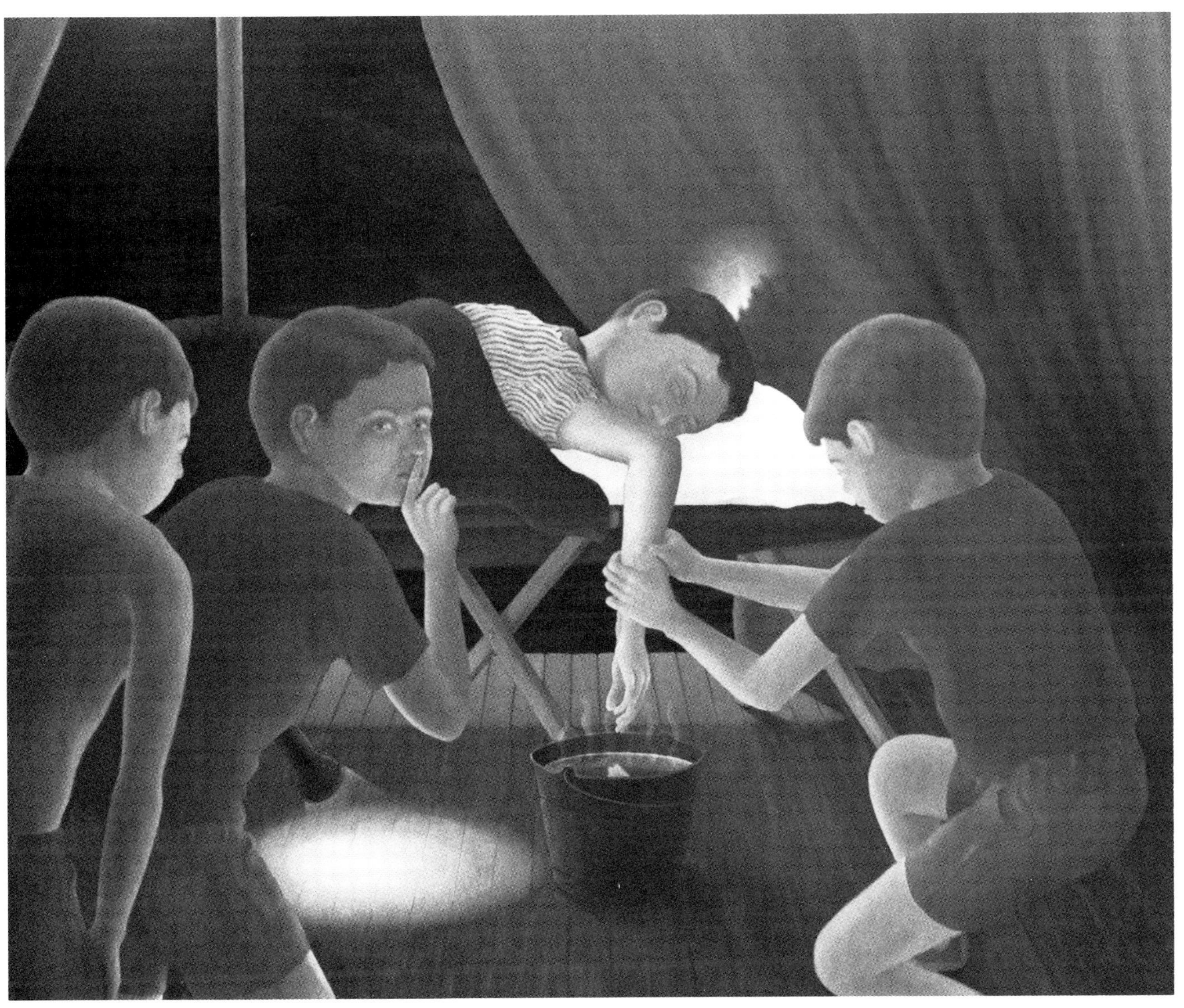

In the Morning 1983
Oil on canvas
66 × 82″
Courtesy the artist and DW Gallery,
Dallas, Texas

Gael Stack

1941
Born, Chicago, Illinois
1970
B.F.A., University of Illinois,
Champaign-Urbana
1972
M.F.A., Southern Illinois University,
Carbondale

The artist has taught at several
universities, including the University of
Wisconsin, LaCrosse, and, since 1979,
the University of Houston, Texas, where
she is an associate professor. She lives
and works in Houston.

Awards

1982
Individual Artists' Fellowship,
National Endowment for the Arts

Selected Solo Exhibitions

1972
Mitchell Gallery, Carbondale, Illinois
1974
The Graphics Gallery, San Francisco,
California
1975-1978
Meredith Long and Company, Houston,
Texas
1977
Art Museum of South Texas, Corpus
Christi
1980-1981
Meredith Long and Company, Houston,
Texas

Selected Group Exhibitions

1970
Mid-States Art Exhibition, Evansville
Museum of Arts and Science, Indiana
1971
16th Mid-South Exhibition, Brooks
Memorial Art Gallery, Memphis,
Tennessee
1972
15th Annual Art Unlimited, Downey
Museum of Art, California
17th Annual Mid-South Exhibition,
Brooks Memorial Art Gallery, Memphis,
Tennessee
1973
*Ball State 19th Annual Drawing and
Small Sculpture Show,* Ball State
University, Muncie, Indiana
1974
*8th Annual National Drawing and Small
Sculpture Show,* Del Mar College,
Corpus Christi, Texas
*16th Annual National Exhibition of Prints
and Drawings,* Oklahoma Art Center,
Norman
Some Other Artists, Alley Theater,
Houston, Texas
1975
Meredith Long and Company, Houston,
Texas
1975 Houston Area Exhibition, Sarah
Campbell Blaffer Gallery, University of
Houston, Texas
1976
New Acquisitions: Works on Paper, The
Museum of Fine Arts, Houston, Texas
1977
Moody Gallery, Houston, Texas
1978
7 x 9, N.A.M.E. Gallery, Chicago, Illinois
(circulated)
1978
Southern Illinois University, Carbondale
1979
Doors, Houston Festival, Texas
(circulated)
FIRE!, Contemporary Arts Museum,
Houston, Texas
Miniatures, Lawndale Annex, University
of Houston, Texas

1980
Houston Annual Exhibition,
Sarah Campbell Blaffer Gallery,
University of Houston, Texas
Texas Artists Invitational, Contemporary
Arts Center, New Orleans, Louisiana
1981
*4 Painters: Jones, Smith, Stack,
Utterback,* Contemporary Arts Museum,
Houston, Texas
*19 Artists-Emergent Americans: 1981
Exxon National Exhibition,* The Solomon
R. Guggenheim Museum, New York City
1982
Americans on Paper, Meredith Long and
Company, Houston, Texas
Art from Houston in Norway,
Stavanger Kunstforening, Norway
New Accessions: Texas Artists, The
Museum of Fine Arts, Houston, Texas
1982
Galerie Simonne Stern, New Orleans,
Louisiana
Texas on Paper, Contemporary Arts
Museum, Houston, Texas (circulated)
1983
Saltzburger Kunstverein, Austria, *Eleven
Houston Artists* (circulated)

Selected References

Contemporary Arts Museum, Houston,
Texas. *FIRE!,* Feb. 16-Apr. 15, 1979. Essay
by James Surls.

Contemporary Arts Museum, Houston,
Texas. *4 Painters: Jones, Smith, Stack,
Utterback,* Oct. 10-Nov. 29, 1981.
Introduction and essays by Linda L.
Cathcart and Marti Mayo.

The Solomon R. Guggenheim Museum,
New York City. *19 Artists-Emergent
Americans: 1981 Exxon National
Exhibition,* Jan. 30-Apr. 5, 1981.
Introduction by Peter Frank.

Stavanger Kunstforening, Norway. *Art
from Houston in Norway,* June 3-28,
1982. Introduction by David Brauer.

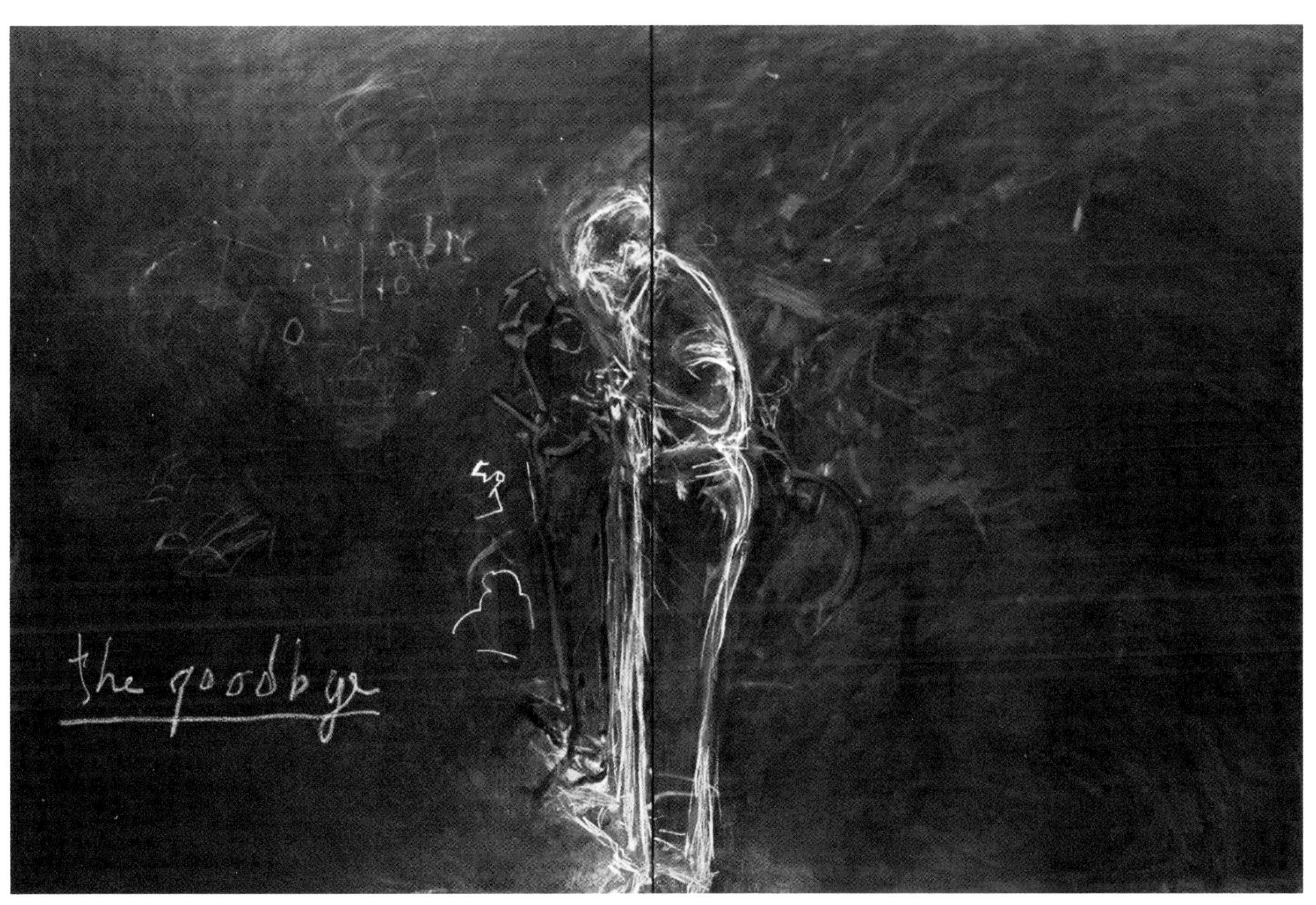

The Goodbye 1983
Mixed media on canvas
52¼ × 80½":
2 panels, each 52¼ × 40¼"
Courtesy the artist and
Janie C. Lee Gallery,
Houston, Texas

Earl Staley

1938
Born, Oak Park, Illinois
1960
B.A., Illinois Wesleyan University, Bloomington
1963
M.F.A., University of Arkansas, Fayetteville

The artist is on leave from the University of St. Thomas in Houston, Texas, where he has taught since 1969. He presently lives and works in Houston and Rome, Italy.

Awards

1975, 1977
Individual Artists' Fellowship, National Endowment for the Arts
1981
Prix de Rome, American Academy of Arts and Letters

Selected Solo Exhibitions

1965
Downstairs Gallery, St. Louis, Missouri
1967
Louisiana Gallery, Houston, Texas
Sewall Art Gallery, Rice University, Houston, Texas
1970
Meredith Long and Company, Houston, Texas
1972
David Gallery, Houston, Texas
1974-1975
Texas Gallery, Houston
1977
Art Museum of South Texas, Corpus Christi
Texas Gallery, Houston
1978
Texas Gallery, Houston
1980
Contemporary Arts Museum, Houston, Texas
Little Egypt Enterprises, Houston, Texas
Watson/de Nagy and Company, Houston, Texas

1981
Phyllis Kind Gallery, New York City
Watson/de Nagy and Company, Houston, Texas
1982
Sewall Art Gallery, Rice University, Houston, Texas
1983
Phyllis Kind Gallery, New York City
Watson/de Nagy and Company, Houston, Texas

Selected Group Exhibitions

1958-1960
Bloomington Illinois Art Association
1962
Oklahoma Museum of Art, Oklahoma City
1964
Brooks Memorial Art Gallery, Memphis, Tennessee
1966
Kansas City Art Institute, Missouri
1970
A Clean Well-Lighted Place, Austin, Texas
1973
Contemporary Arts Museum, Houston, Texas
1974
The Museum of Fine Arts, Houston, Texas
1975
Houston Area Exhibition, Sarah Campbell Blaffer Gallery, University of Houston, Texas
La Jolla Museum of Contemporary Art, California
1975 Biennial Exhibition, Whitney Museum of American Art, New York City
1976
Institute of Contemporary Art, University of Pennsylvania, Philadelphia
Texas Gallery, Houston
1976-1979
University of St. Thomas, Houston, Texas
1977
Houston Area Exhibition, Sarah Campbell Blaffer Gallery, University of Houston, Texas
1978
"Bad" Painting, The New Museum, New York City

1979
FIRE!, Contemporary Arts Museum, Houston, Texas
Made in Texas, Archer M. Huntington Gallery, University Art Museum, The University of Texas at Austin
The Museum of Fine Arts, Houston, Texas
The 1970's: New American Painting organized by The New Museum, New York City, for the U.S. International Communications Agency (circulated in Eastern Europe)
1980
Houston Area Exhibition, Sarah Campbell Blaffer Gallery, University of Houston, Texas
1980 New Orleans Triennial, New Orleans Museum of Art, Louisiana
1981
A Texas Group Show, Charles Cowles Gallery, New York City
Directions 1981, Hirshhorn Museum and Sculpture Garden, Smithsonian Institution, Washington, D.C. (circulated)
1982
Art from Houston in Norway, Stavanger Kunstforening, Norway
Texas on Paper, Contemporary Arts Museum, Houston, Texas (circulated)

Selected References

Whitney Museum of American Art, New York City. *1975 Biennial Exhibition,* Jan. 20-Apr. 9, 1975. Foreword by Tom Armstrong.

The New Museum, New York City. *"Bad" Painting,* Jan. 14-Feb. 28, 1978, Essay by Marcia Tucker.

Archer M. Huntington Gallery, University Art Museum, The University of Texas at Austin. *Made in Texas,* May 20-Aug. 26, 1979. Introduction by Becky Duval Reese. Essays by Janet Kutner and Tom Livesay.

Hirshhorn Museum and Sculpture Garden, Smithsonian Institution, Washington, D.C. *Directions 1981,* Feb. 12-May 3, 1981. Foreword by Abram Lerner. Introduction by Miranda McClintic.

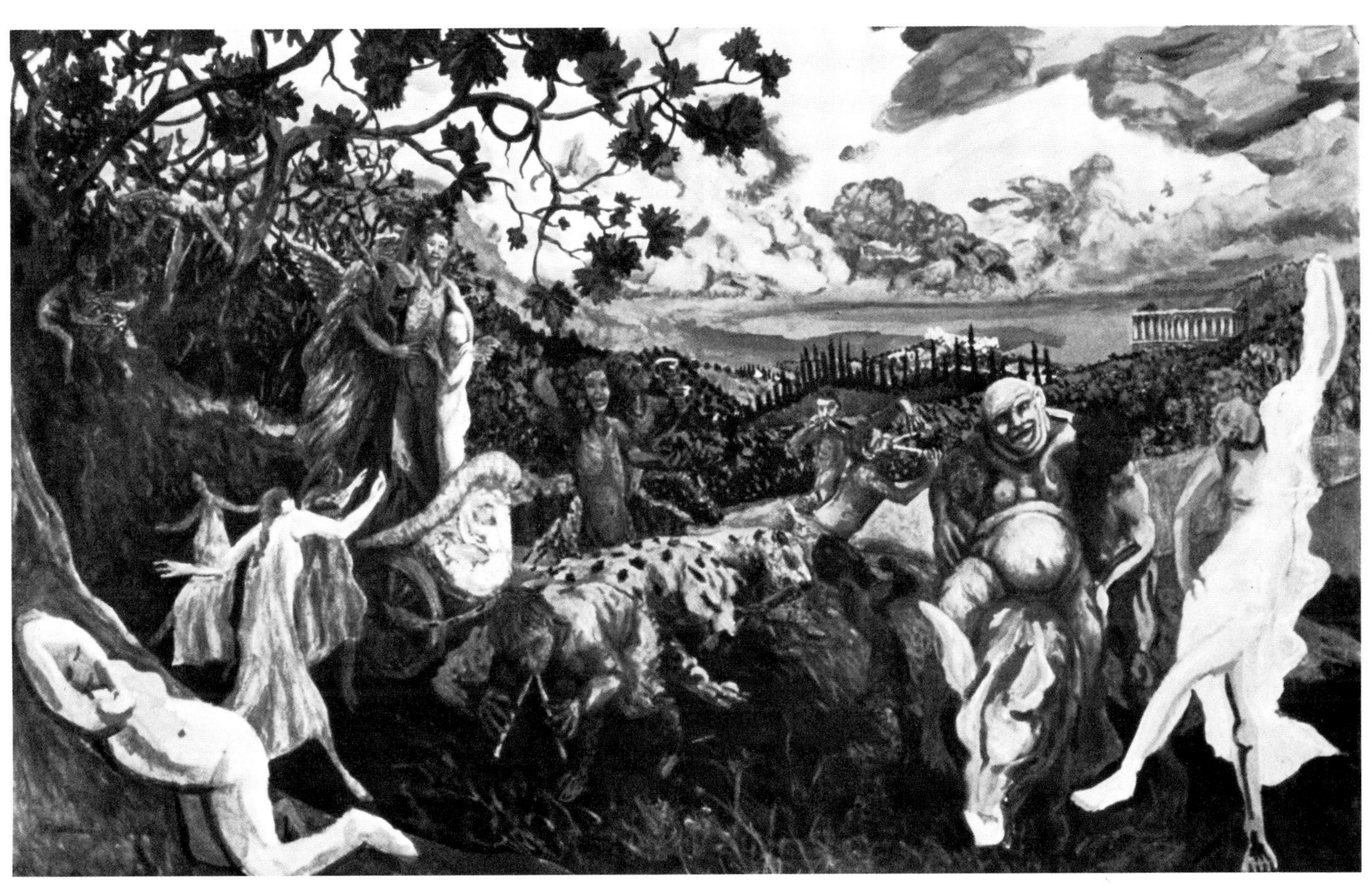

The Triumph of Bacchus 1982
Acrylic on canvas
51½ × 83½″
Courtesy the artist and
Watson/de Nagy and Company,
Houston, Texas

Richard Stout

1934
Born, Beaumont, Texas
1957
B.F.A., The School of The Art Institute of Chicago, Illinois
1969
M.F.A., The University of Texas at Austin

The artist has been an associate professor at the University of Houston, Texas, since 1967. He lives and works in Houston.

Selected Solo Exhibitions

1959
The New Arts Gallery, Houston, Texas
1961
Beaumont Art Museum, Texas
1963-1981
Meredith Long and Company, Houston, Texas
1964
Kansas City Art Institute, Missouri
1966
Marion Koogler McNay Art Institute, San Antonio, Texas
1971
Marion Koogler McNay Art Institute, San Antonio, Texas
1973
Tyler Museum of Art, Texas
Contemporary Arts Museum, Houston, Texas
1980
Jurgen Schwinebraden, Berlin, West Germany
1983
Meredith Long and Company, Houston, Texas
Touchstone Gallery, New York City

Selected Group Exhibitions

1953
Art Academy of Cincinnati, Ohio
1956
The 1014 Art Center, Chicago, Illinois
1958
Beaumont Art Museum, Texas
1960
Annual Exhibition, The Butler Institute of Art, Youngstown, Ohio
Artists' Annual, Isaac Delgado Museum of Art, New Orleans, Louisiana
1961
Contemporary Arts Museum, Houston, Texas
1971
The Other Coast, California State College, Long Beach.
1973
Three Americans, Texas Fine Arts Association (circulated)
1974
Abstract Painting in Houston, The Museum of Fine Arts, Houston, Texas
1977
Houston Area Exhibition, Sarah Campbell Blaffer Gallery, University of Houston, Texas
International Art Fair, Cologne, West Germany
1979
Achenbach and Kimmerich, Dusseldorf, West Germany
Doors, Houston Festival, Houston, Texas
1980
Eros, Julius Hummel Kunsthandlung, Vienna, Austria
Gallerie Thommen, Basel, Switzerland
1981
Gallerie de Arti Pellegrino, Bologna, Italy
1982
Art from Houston in Norway, Stavanger Kunstforening, Norway
1983
1983 New Orleans Triennial, New Orleans Museum of Art, Louisiana
Eleven Houston Artists, Saltzburger Kunstverein, Austria (circulated)

Selected References

Sarah Campbell Blaffer Gallery, University of Houston, Texas. *1977 Houston Area Exhibition.* Oct. 8-Nov. 10, 1977. Introduction and notes by William A. Robinson.

Peter Weiermair and Benedict Press, Munsterschwarzach, Austria. *Eleven Houston Artists,* 1983-1984. Essay by William A. Camfield.

Stavanger Kunstforening, Norway. *Art from Houston in Norway,* June 3-28, 1982. Introduction by David Brauer.

New Orleans Musem of Art, Louisiana. *1983 New Orleans Triennial,* Apr. 8-May 22, 1983. Introduction by William A. Fagaly. Essay by Linda L. Cathcart.

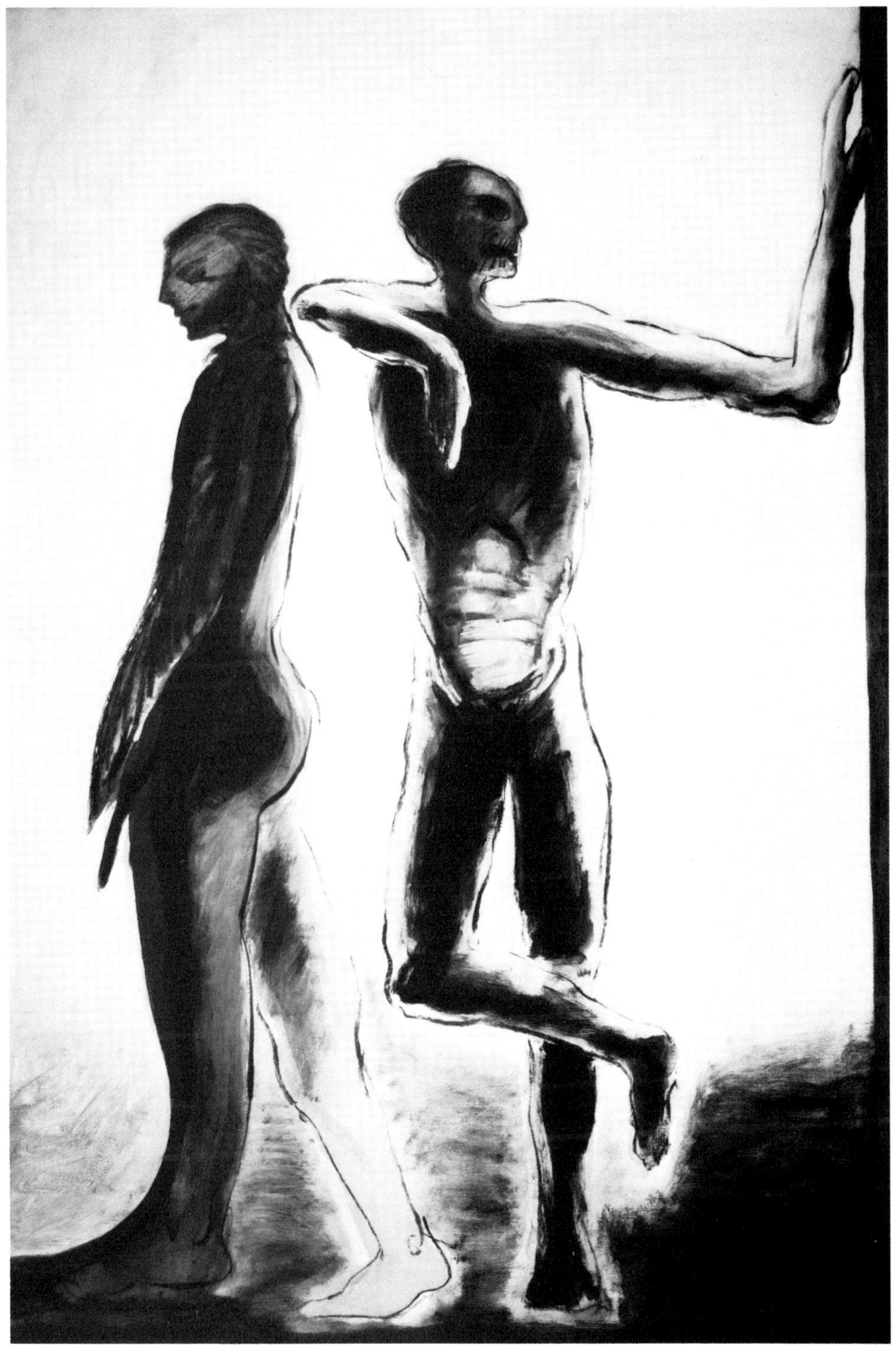

Brothers 1982
Acrylic on canvas
72 × 50″
Courtesy the artist and
Meredith Long and Company,
Houston, Texas

James Surls

1943
Born, Terrell, Texas
1966
B.S., Sam Houston State College, Huntsville, Texas
1969
M.F.A., Cranbrook Academy of Art, Bloomfield Hills, Michigan

The artist has taught at several universities, including Southern Methodist University, Dallas, Texas. From 1978 to 1982, he was an associate professor of Art at the University of Houston, Texas. He lives and works in Splendora, Texas.

Selected Solo Exhibitions

1974
Delahunty Gallery, Dallas, Texas
Tyler Museum of Art, Texas
1975
James Surls: Sculptor, Contemporary Arts Museum, Houston, Texas
1977
Delahunty Gallery, Dallas, Texas
1979
Delahunty Gallery, Dallas, Texas
Robinson Galleries, Houston, Texas
1980
Allan Frumkin Gallery, New York City
1981
Daniel Weinberg Gallery, San Francisco, California
Delahunty Gallery, Dallas, Texas
1982
Allan Frumkin Gallery, New York City
Akron Art Museum, Ohio
The Saint Louis Art Museum, Missouri

Selected Group Exhibitions

1965
14th Annual Painting and Sculpture Exhibition, Beaumont Art Museum, Texas
1967
Bloomfield Art Association Sculpture Show, Bloomfield Hills, Michigan

1968
14th Annual Drawing and Small Sculpture Show, Muncie, Indiana
1970
11th Annual Painting and Sculpture Exhibition, Oklahoma Art Center, Oklahoma City
1971
14th Annual Delta Art Exhibition, Little Rock, Arkansas
1973
Tarrant County Annual, Fort Worth Art Museum, Texas
1974
8th Annual National Drawing and Small Sculpture Exhibition, Del Mar College, Corpus Christi, Texas
12/Texas, Contemporary Arts Museum, Houston, Texas
1975
Artists Make Toys, Art Museum of South Texas, Corpus Christi
The Dog Show, University Gallery, Southern Methodist University, Dallas, Texas
Exchange: DFW/SFO, Fort Worth Art Museum, Texas (circulated)
1976
Tex/Lax: Texas in L.A., Union Gallery, California State University, Los Angeles
1977
Installations in Corner Spaces, Fort Worth Art Museum, Texas
Nine Artists: Theodoron Awards, The Solomon R. Guggenheim Museum, New York City
1979
FIRE!, Contemporary Arts Museum, Houston, Texas
Made in Texas, Archer M. Huntington Gallery, University Art Museum, The University of Texas at Austin
1979 Biennial Exhibition, Whitney Museum of American Art, New York City
1980
First Person Singular: Recent Response, Tyler Museum of Art, Texas
Self-Portraiture, Pratt Institute Gallery, New York City

1980
Surls and Locke, University Center Art Gallery, Louisiana State University, Shreveport
10 Abstract Sculptures, Max Hutchinson Gallery, New York City
The Texas Invitational, Contemporary Arts Center, New Orleans, Louisiana
Two from Texas, Galerie Simonne Stern, New Orleans, Louisiana
1981
The Image of the House in Contemporary Art, Lawndale Annex, University of Houston, Texas
1982
Art from Houston in Norway, Stavanger Kunstforening, Norway
1983
Fact and Fiction: New Work by James Surls, Roy Fridge, Ed Blackburn, Vernon Fisher, Aspen Center for the Visual Arts, Colorado

Selected References

Contemporary Arts Museum, Houston, Texas. *James Surls: Sculptor*, Mar. 29-Apr. 30, 1975. Essay by Michael Samuels.

Whitney Museum of American Art, New York City. *1979 Biennial Exhibition*, Feb. 14-Apr. 1, 1979. Foreword by John G. Hanhardt. Essays by Barbara Haskell, Richard Marshall, Mark Segal and Patterson Sims.

Archer M. Huntington Gallery, University Art Museum, The University of Texas at Austin. *Made in Texas*, May 20-Aug. 26, 1979. Introduction by Becky Duval Reese. Essays by Janet Kutner and Tom Livesay.

Lawndale Annex, University of Houston, Texas. *The Image of the House in Contemporary Art*, Nov. 8-Dec. 4, 1981. Foreword by Charmaine Locke. Essay by William Simon.

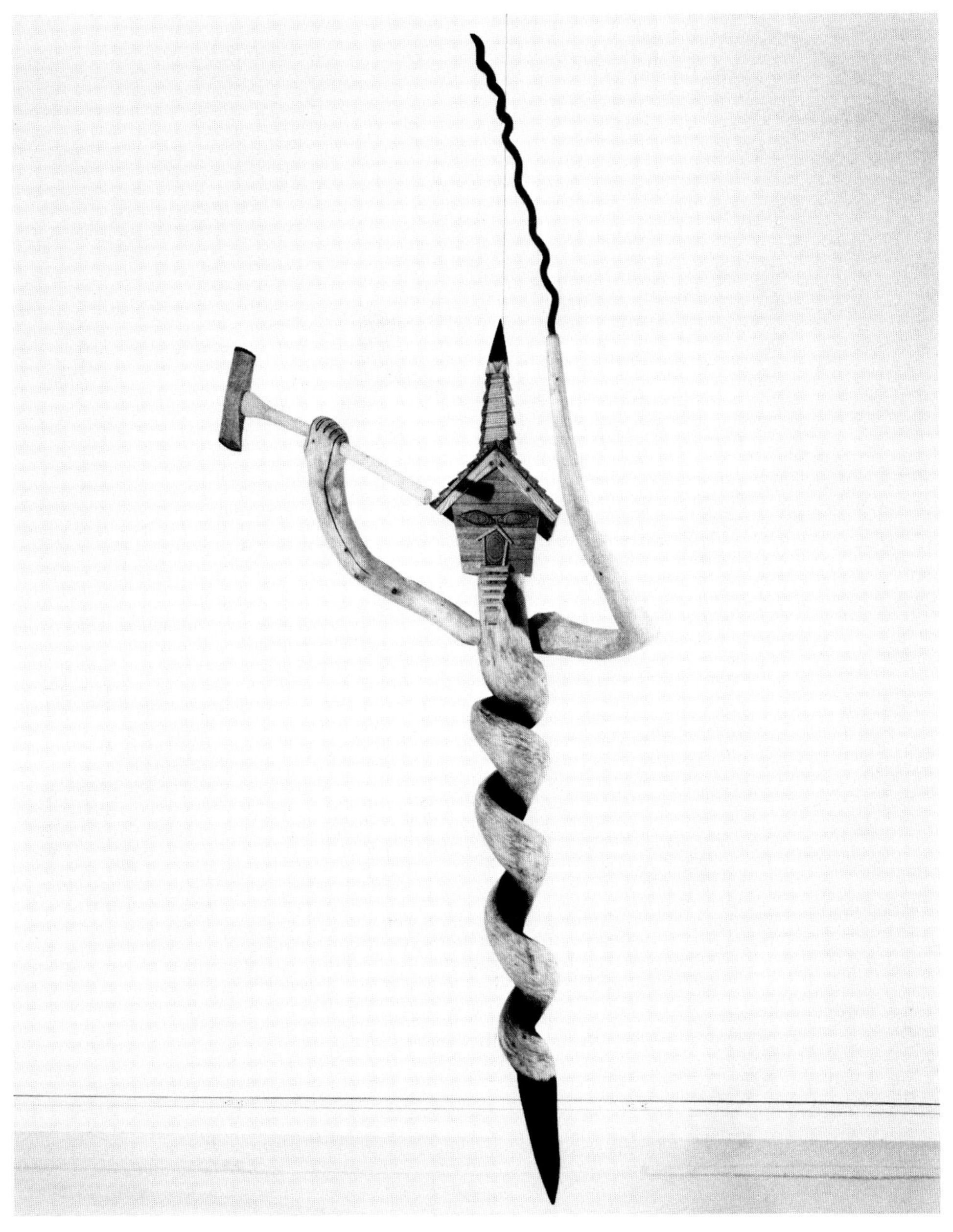

Me, the Axe, the Wand 1982
Pine, mahogany, oak, hickory and rattan
125½ × 44 × 26"
Courtesy the artist and
Delahunty Gallery,
Dallas, Texas

Russell Warren

1951
Born, Washington, D.C.
1973
B.F.A., University of New Mexico, Albuquerque
1977
M.F.A., The University of Texas at San Antonio

Since 1978, the artist has been an assistant professor of Art at Davidson College in North Carolina, where he lives and works.

Selected Solo Exhibitions

1972
Old Town Studio, Albuquerque, New Mexico
1975
University of St. Thomas, Houston, Texas
1977
San Antonio Museum of Art, Texas
The University of Texas at San Antonio
1978
Store Front Gallery, Tampa Bay Arts Council, Tampa, Florida
1979
Art Gallery, Davidson College, North Carolina
1980
University of North Carolina, Charlotte
1981
High Point Arts Council, North Carolina
Phyllis Kind Gallery, New York City
1982
Phyllis Kind Gallery, Chicago, Illinois
Phyllis Kind Gallery, New York City

Selected Group Exhibitions

1975
Southeastern Texas Collective, Beaumont Art Museum, Texas
1975 Artists Biennial, New Orleans Museum of Art, Louisiana
1976
Artists Invitational, Beaumont Art Museum, Texas
Christmas Print and Drawing Exhibition, San Antonio Museum of Art, Texas

1977
Amarillo Art Competition, Amarillo Art Center, Texas
Bosch Bash, University of St. Thomas, Houston, Texas
Houston Area Exhibition, Sarah Campbell Blaffer Gallery, University of Houston, Texas
1979
Appalachian National Drawing Competition, Farthing Art Gallery, Boone, North Carolina
Biennial, Mint Museum of Art, Charlotte, North Carolina
Miniatures, Lawndale Annex, University of Houston, Texas
Rutgers Drawing '79, Rutgers University, Camden, New Jersey
1980
48th Painting and Sculpture, Southeast Center for Contemporary Art, Winston-Salem, North Carolina
The Dog Show, Collectors Gallery, North Carolina Museum of Art, Raleigh
1980 New Orleans Triennial, New Orleans Museum of Art, Louisiana
Tragicomedy, Mystery, and Humor, North Carolina Museum of Art, Raleigh
1981
Currents: A New Mannerism, Jacksonville Art Museum, Florida
Figures: Forms and Expressions, Albright-Knox Art Gallery, CEPA Gallery and HALLWALLS, Buffalo, New York
1981 Biennial Exhibition, Whitney Museum of American Art, New York City
1982
Agitated Figures: The New Emotionalism, HALLWALLS, Buffalo, New York (circulated)
Beast, Institute for Art and Urban Resources, P.S. 1, Long Island City, New York
The Human Figure in Contemporary Art, Contemporary Arts Center, New Orleans, Louisiana
New Painting I: America, Middendorf/Lane Gallery, Washington, D.C.
Painting and Sculpture Today, Indianapolis Museum of Art, Indiana

1983
Intoxication, Monique Knowlton Gallery, New York City
Painting in the South, Virginia Museum of Fine Arts, Richmond
Phyllis Kind Gallery, New York City

Selected References

New Orleans Museum of Art, Louisiana. *1975 Artists Biennial,* June 20-July 20, 1975. Foreword by E. John Bullard. Essay by Jane Livingston.

New Orleans Museum of Art, Louisiana. *1980 New Orleans Triennial,* Oct. 3-Nov. 16, 1980. Introduction by William A. Fagaly. Essay by Marcia Tucker.

Whitney Museum of American Art, New York City. *1981 Biennial Exhibition,* Jan. 20-Apr. 19, 1981. Foreword by Tom Armstrong. Essays by Barbara Haskell, Richard Marshall and Patterson Sims.

Albright-Knox Art Gallery, CEPA Gallery and HALLWALLS, Buffalo, New York. *Figures: Forms and Expressions,* Nov. 20, 1981-Jan. 3, 1982. Introduction and essays by Robert Collignon, William Currie, G. Roger Denson, Biff Henrich, Susan Krane and Charlotta Kotik.

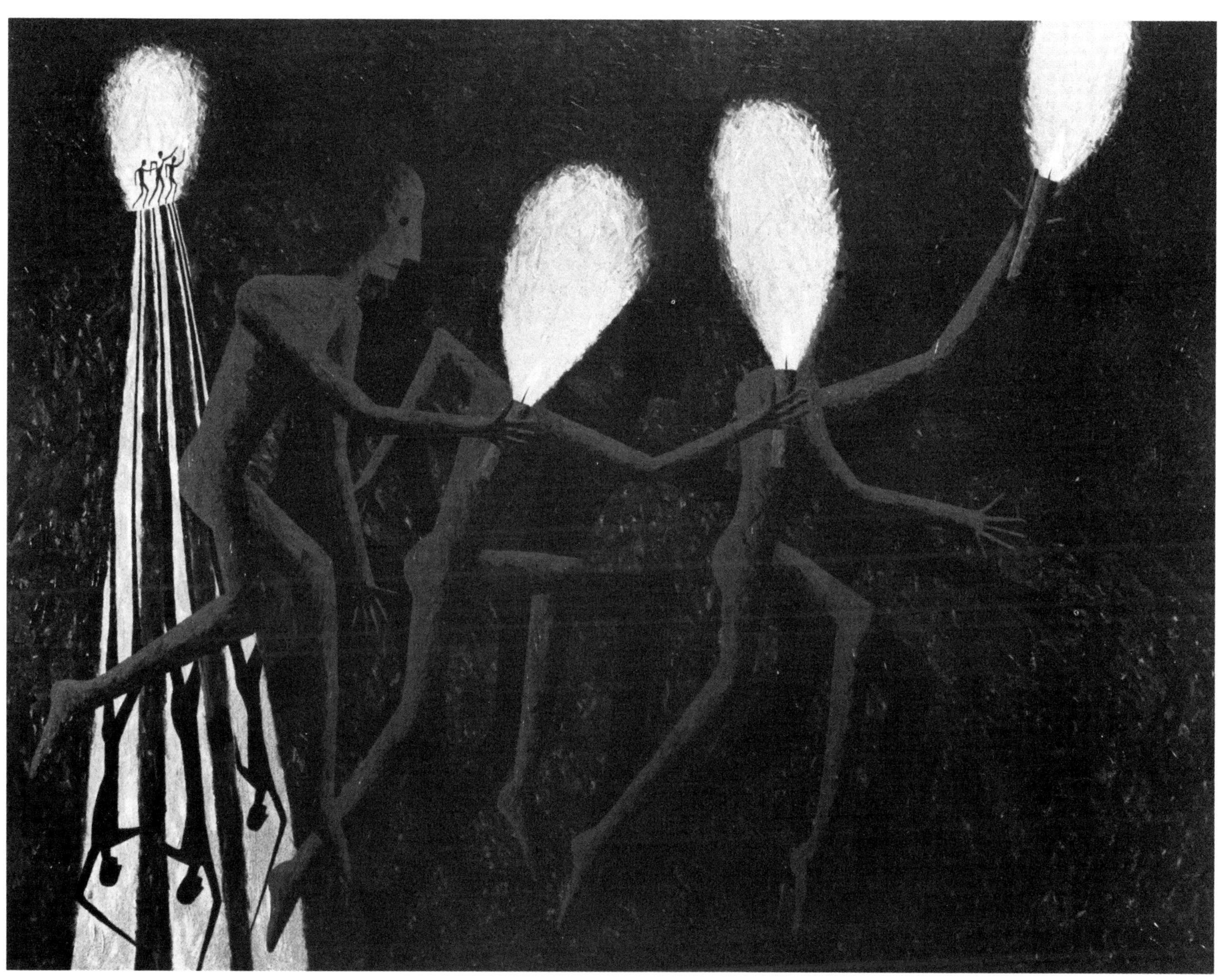

Parade 1983
Acrylic on canvas
55 × 72″
Courtesy the artist and
Phyllis Kind Gallery, New York City

Susan Whyne

1946
Born, New York City
1968
B.F.A., Cooper Union School of Art and Architecture, New York City
1974
M.F.A., San Francisco State University, California

The artist has been an assistant professor at The University of Texas at Austin since 1977. She lives and works in Austin.

Awards

1980
Individual Artists' Fellowship, National Endowment for the Arts

Selected Solo Exhibitions

1974
Candy Store Gallery, Folsom, California

Selected Group Exhibitions

1971
Paint on Paper, San Francisco Art Institute, California
1973
San Francisco Art Commission Gallery, California
Sonoma State College, California

1974
Bay Area Studio Sampler, San Francisco, California
Bay Area Women Artists, Evergreen State College, Olympia, Washington
Summer '75, University Art Museum, University of California, Berkeley
1976
Surface and Image, Walnut Creek Civic Arts Center, California
1977
Cityscapes — San Francisco and Los Angeles, Fine Arts Museum of San Francisco, California
Touching All Things — 35 Bay Area Women Artists, Walnut Creek Civic Arts Center, California
1978
Works on Paper: Southwest 1978, Dallas Museum of Fine Arts, Texas
1979
Austin Contemporary Art, Laguna Gloria Art Museum, Austin, Texas
Miniatures, Lawndale Annex, University of Houston, Texas
New Works, Laguna Gloria Art Museum, Austin, Texas
Texas Artists Invitational Narrative Show, Corpus Christi State University, Texas
1980
Emerging Artists, Mattingly Baker Gallery, Dallas, Texas
1982
Austin Contemporary Art, Dougherty Cultural Arts Center, Austin, Texas
Here and Now, Dougherty Cultural Arts Center, Austin, Texas
1983
1983 New Orleans Triennial, New Orleans Museum of Art, Louisiana

Selected References

New Orleans Museum of Art, Louisiana. *1983 New Orleans Triennial,* Apr. 8-May 22, 1983. Introduction by William A. Fagaly. Essay by Linda L. Cathcart.

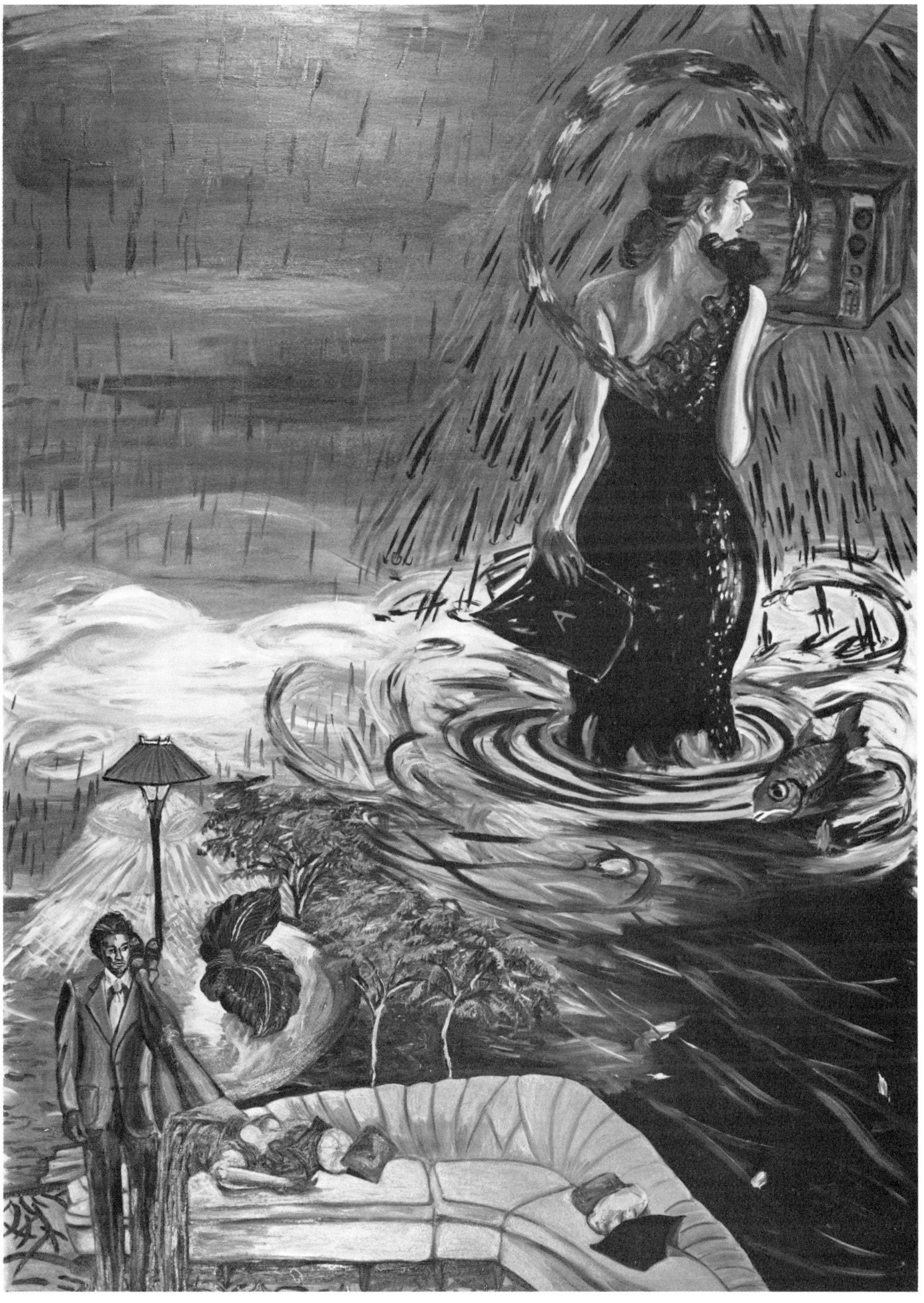

Flamenco and the Nic-Nac Man 1983
Oil on canvas
90 × 65″
Courtesy the artist

Photography Credits

Jerrie Crabb, Houston, Texas, p. 43.
D W Gallery, Dallas, Texas, p. 67.
Delahunty Gallery, Dallas, Texas, pp. 16, 41, 59, 75.
Steve Dennie, Dallas, Texas, pp. 59, 75.
Pat Donley, Davidson, North Carolina, p. 77.
Rick Gardner, Houston, Texas, pp. 8, 31, 51.
Vincent Gargotta, Houston, Texas, pp. 25, 69.
Janie C. Lee Gallery, Houston, Texas, pp. 25, 69.
Meredith Long and Company, Houston, Texas, p. 73.
Middendorf Gallery, Washington, D.C., pp. 13, 39.
Moody Gallery, Houston, Texas, pp. 33, 43.
Texas Gallery, Houston, Texas, p. 29.
Tyler Museum of Art, pp. 8, 15, 31, 57.
Watson/de Nagy and Company, p. 71.
Zindman/Fremont, New York, New York, p. 65.

Design by **Creel Morrell Inc.**; Houston, Texas
1000 copies printed by **Brandt & Lawson**; Houston, Texas
Typesetting by **Encom Graphics**; Houston, Texas